Brian's
To
Working With Spirit

by
Rhiannon Faulkner

Say It With Angels Publishing

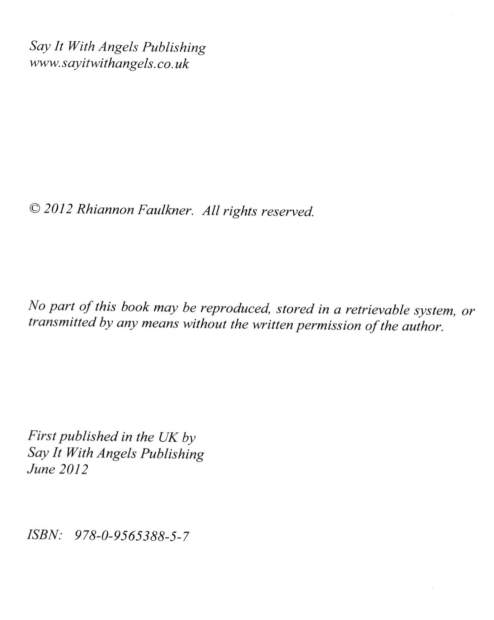

Say It With Angels Publishing
www.sayitwithangels.co.uk

First published in the UK by
Say It With Angels Publishing
June 2012

ISBN: 978-0-9565388-5-7

Dedication

For all the people who have ever said to Rhiannon, "I wish I could do what you do, but I can't because I'm not gifted."

This one's for you guys.

Love Bri x

"So, You Wanna Be Psychic?"

My name is Brian Copthorne.

I am the guide that you all know as the little Irish dwarf that works with Rhiannon Faulkner; she's the lassie who created the Faulkner Tarot Deck for my fellow friends here in the other realm. She has also created my very own deck – Brian's Deck.

Now, I have badgered the boss lady, as I affectionately call her, (trust me, she is bossy), to write this book for me. I think it is about time that one of us put into simple words how we, in spirit, need you to co-operate with us.

Come on! It's way past the dark ages. You are all aware of 'another world', 'life after death' and 'guidance from above', yet not a lot of you seem to get the formula right......

My intention is to help you wonderful lot, who are reading this, to build the same bond with your guides. Let's smash out the myth that you have to be a 'special and gifted' person to connect with your guides. Anyone and everyone is capable of doing this, so sit back, get comfy and read my advice. Then, walk away, have a think and, after a little sulk and a bit of head scratching, pick up the book and read it again. It will sink in eventually, honest.

Rhiannon and I work in a different way to how she works with her other guides. We are friends. We have broken down the barriers, gotten past the fact that we don't even live in the same realm, have achieved a true friendship and have found a bond, as a result of being brought together to work. My wife and kids know her as 'Daddy's work' and her kids have accepted me as 'Mummy's weird friend'. Yes, that's right; I have kids over here, currently seven of the blighters, if you must know. You see, I am in a different realm to where your loved ones go to after they have passed.

It's not just Heaven and Earth ya know....

I was sent to Rhiannon this time round, as we have known each other from a long time ago. We used to be married to each other in a past life. So, you see, you can experience life in different realms. We have been here in my world together and were also together in your world, once upon a time. This makes me very qualified in knowing how to handle the woman – I know everything about her, the good the bad and the downright ugly.

Why do we have to work together again? Well, this time Rhiannon and I have agreed to help each other one last time. We are working to educate people about the bigger story and we are here to offer support to others. This lesson has been tough on the old boss. You see, to be able to fully understand her job, she has had to experience the loss of her husband at a young age, to cancer. She had to see death and experience the grief process personally. I was sent to keep her sane, to carry both her and her husband through the parting and then, to support her on her life path afterwards.

This book is my way of getting my job done – using Rhiannon to write for me. I want to teach you all to be able to channel your guides so that you will be able to better your lives and the lives of others, who come to you for help.

Common Myths
Things You May Have Heard and Even Believed!

"Only gifted people are psychic."

"It's hereditary."

"You can't believe in God and also be psychic."

"It's wrong."

"You will go to Hell."

"You can't channel if you smoke or drink too much caffeine."

"You have to meditate every day."

"It takes years to be good at it."

What a load of rubbish…….. Shall we begin?

CHAPTER 1
Going Back to Basics

When you work with guides properly, you become a pure channel. Imagine yourself as an empty tube. We shout through one end and our words come out of your mouth unchanged – exactly the way it sounded when it first left our lips, but in your voice.

However, to become a pure channel you have to remove all blocks first, otherwise our words become distorted - a bit like Chinese whispers, or even sometimes, like a downright lie. So, how do you make sure you are this pure empty channel for us to work with?

Well firstly, believing and knowing that it is not YOU speaking, helps.

Think of a spokesperson on the TV giving a grand impressive speech, which is aired on the worldwide news. Does the translator in the corner of the screen, who is presenting the words in a different language, or the guy working hard to type the subtitles on the screen, get the credit for the speech? No! He is just passing on the message. That's exactly what you guys do when speaking for spirit.

So, let's take a stroll through this list of potential blocks…

- **Fear**
- **Lack of Self Worth**
- **Ego**
- **Anger**
- **Gains**

Mmmmm.... I bet on first glance at the list you feel that you have passed with flying colours and have declared yourself ready to go. Now let's go through them one by one.

Learning how to become a channel is sometimes a painful journey. This happens as you work to rid yourself of all your deepest, darkest fears and problems. They are often ones that you wish didn't exist and that you would rather ignore, but you are human this time round, so how on earth do you expect to be perfect? Stop being so hard on yourself – you have taken the first step in the right direction already.

An emotion, to us over here, is like a cloud of thick smog that we cannot get through. It is like a brick wall that we need to smash through before we can even begin to see the real you.

Fear

This is a very common emotion to have.

Fear of not being able to succeed.
Fear of not being able to do something.
Fear of not being good enough and becoming a laughing stock to mankind.

Mmmmm, so that's the little devil called ego kicking in. What will people say? They will think I have gone mad. "What if the message I pass on is wrong?"

So, what if I remind you that it is not YOU giving the messages? Instead you are channelling the messages from a guide in spirit. Does that take the pressure off you? It should. How can you be afraid of not being good at something, when it is not you doing it in the first place?

Fear of the unknown is another factor – being scared of the voices you are about to hear, or being scared of the faces you might actually see, or even being scared of the message you are being told to give.

Well let me reassure you that your guides do not, under any circumstances, want to scare you off. They know better than you do yourself when you are ready to see, or hear, or both. Trust that they will make it happen at the right time for you.

Fear often blocks Rhiannon from seeing me. This happens when she is simply scared of hearing advice and she pre-empts what my guidance is going to be, or she thinks she knows what's going to happen next.

Rhiannon has a real issue with this one. She trusts my words implicitly, when passing on messages for other people, but she struggles to listen when it's for her personally.

Lack of self worth

"They wouldn't want to use me, I am not good enough."
"I am not worthy."
"I am not clever enough."
"I wouldn't know what to do."
"I can't do it."

Oh come on! Seriously? You were good enough to be born into this world and trusted to live a life here. Do you still believe that you are nothing – unloved and unwanted? Get over it! God created you – why would he just leave you here? Get ready to stand up and be counted.

So you really think you can't do this channelling lark? Let's move on and come back to this one after having discussed the other negative reasons on the list.

Ego

Laughing the whole way here. Not got an ego? Really? How about when you have succeeded at something and have done the punch in the air? That feeling of elation and sheer pride is wonderful and completely natural. However, what about when it doesn't go away and becomes food for the ego? Ego is a problem for all human beings – don't beat yourself up about it, just learn to curb it. It's a natural part of being a human being.

So, how do we curb the ego when working with spirit? Well let's ponder on this one. How can you take the sole credit for something that took a team effort? You and your guides worked together, as a team.

Now, let's turn that ego into pride. Be proud that you were an important team member, necessary to get that message from spirit out to the earth world. It's a wonderful thing to take pride in your work, but don't let me catch you saying "I am really good", or "I am a brilliant psychic". It's the 'I' word that gets you into trouble. Instead say "Thank you" to your guide when a message has been proved to be accurate. Say "Thank you" to your guide when the message has helped someone. Say "Thank you" for being included in the process. This will train you to pass over responsibility to your guide and it will curb your ego instantly.

Then there are some that say "I have been hearing and seeing spirit since I was tiny, it comes naturally to me and I don't have to learn how to do it." Wow! That's an ego talking, if ever I heard one. It

8

came naturally to you to walk and talk too, but someone had to guide you through the basics first, you know. They had to teach you how to put one foot in front of the other and not one on top of the other. Someone had to teach you how to put a spoon in your mouth. Remember, there is nothing wrong with having to learn. In fact, that's why you are here in this world – to learn.

Also, don't forget that channelling came naturally to every single human being in the world too – but some get complacent. Just because you walk upright, doesn't mean to say that you don't ever walk in the wrong direction and lose your footing. Get my drift?

You know, the damage people do when they channel through ego is horrendous, for us in spirit, to watch. Strangely though, the people who are ego driven are also the first ones to blame spirit, if things go wrong. Go figure?

We say, you may indeed be able to channel, but are you channelling the right words, or is the ego telling you what to hear and say? However, let us take a little look at the circumstances when people say this. Normally you will find that these words are uttered when they are in the presence of fellow 'psychics' and they are trying to rid themselves of opposition and competition. Why? It is because of their fear – their fear of failure. Oh look! You all have the same fears, hopes and dreams. Translated – you are all HUMAN!

So, let's smash the myth that being able to work with spirit is a 'gift' and only certain people have this ability. SMASHED! What a load of rubbish. You guys only use 1/6th of your human brain. What do you think the rest is for? To fill a gap? No. Every single human being is equipped with the ability to work with their guides. Get over yourselves, you are not unique. So, the minute you hear yourself saying "I am a great medium." "I am 100% accurate." "I am never wrong", smack yourself on the head and bring yourself back in line, or your guides will do it for you.

You never hear people bragging that they are unique because they have a head placed on their shoulders, as it's clear that every other human has one of these too.

So, let's start letting everyone know, that being 'psychic' is a common human ability too.

Anger

We just simply cannot get through this one. Anger pushes us away. It is a forceful emotion, fuelled from hate – a very negative emotion, as you well know. Anger at the world, anger at your situation in life, anger at your misfortune or anger at your failure – oh the list carries on. You might as well quit now, if you hang onto this emotion in life. You are doing more harm to yourself than anyone around you. It literally eats you up on the inside. If you can imagine it as a black wall of sticky glue, you will be able to see from our point of view, how difficult it is and near on impossible to get through.

If you have faith and trust, then you will know that there is no point in holding onto anger. Just ask for help to resolve a situation and you will get it in no time at all. Problem solved!

Gains

Be honest, the thought has crossed your mind at some point, that you could make some decent money from working with spirit. That's fine, we understand that you need paper money to survive in your material world, but don't use us now will you? If you only work for monetary gain, or for recognition (it's that damn ego again) – we will stop working with you immediately, then you really will look like a fool, won't ya?

Have you not noticed how you get rewarded by spirit in so many ways when you do your job properly? When you pass on a message for us, so many good things come to you, yet you don't always recognise, or appreciate them. You are stuck on the idea that you're not doing a proper job, unless people pay for your services, there and then. Start noticing what is being brought to you; it is actually bigger and better than your wildest dreams. Say "Thanks" and acknowledge that spirit have rewarded you each and every time.

On the flip side – there are humans who will tell you that you are not to gain financially from working with spirit, at all. Really? So you honestly think that we would take over your life and expect you to work with us, to help people, on a full time basis. As a result, you would not have a chance to hold down another job to ensure your basic living needs are met and yet we would not allow you to be paid? Oh come on now, we know you need to pay your bills in this world. Don't worry, on the occasions when money cannot, or should not be exchanged, we will provide it for you in another way. Trust us – we will not fail you, if you do not fail us.

So we have talked about what you mustn't have, to be able to be a pure channel for spirit to work through, now let us list the things you absolutely need.

- **Trust**
- **Faith**
- **Love**
- **Honesty**

Trust

Trust that we are real, trust that we are working with you. Just believe. Just know. As frustrating as it is not being able to hear our voices, or see us straight away, just trust that we are there guiding you. It takes a long time to learn how to work together – on both sides. We have to learn how to handle you and your quirky ways and you have to become accustomed to our ways. It's a two way relationship you see. It's a bit like steering a boat from our side and a little like you learning to sail the boat with the aid of the wind only – no engine....

Doubt is a killer. It also eats you up on the inside, makes your stomach churn and is very closely linked to that old devil called ego.

Faith

Knowing, (not just hoping), that you are not alone on this path.

A belief in our Creator would be helpful. To be able to work with spirit in the same way that Rhiannon and I do, that is.

Of course there are a lot of successful mediums working with spirit guides who do not believe in God. So go read one of their books then! This book is to help you have a relationship with your guide, just like Rhiannon and I do.

We both know that God is top dog and we work for Him. We both pray to Him for guidance and listen to His instruction very carefully. My job is to force Rhiannon to listen, even when the human emotions get in the way. Team work again, see?

Rhiannon has battled with her traditional church beliefs and her ability to see dead people – this makes the church frown upon her every step of the way. Quite frankly, she is not welcome in most churches, unless of course they think they can sway her beliefs and make a true Christian out of her. They are prepared to forgive her sins...pah! It has taken her years to get over the guilt and lack of self worth, but finally she has realised that God made her just the way she is – including the ability to see the dead people and, it is not a sin to convey with them.

The church has been ruined by man, folks, just remember this. God made us all and wants us to show His existence through our lives and work. Let it shine. I know there are a lot of you who quietly battle with having to choose whether you are a Christian or a Spiritualist, pagan or whatever and try to figure out which box you fit in. You don't belong in a box! Other people might like this idea, but don't waste time giving a toss where you fit into society. You just concentrate on your own faith.

The church, (which does not mean our Creator), has to rule with fear these days to be able to keep going financially. People are waking up and realising that God lives on in your hearts, not in a building. The building is a great place to come and give thanks in groups. To be able to sit in the congregation and pray together is wonderful. Remember you were taught many years ago, by God's son, a fantastic channel Himself, that praying in small groups really has an effect.

Well, when Rhiannon goes to church and prays, I pray with her. We both give thanks, we both ask for help, we share the same faith and the same belief that we work for the same 'Boss'. Even from different realms, from different worlds, we come together and pray.

Some of you have been so let down by the people who run the religious organisations, that you have changed beliefs. It doesn't matter you know, where you go or where you sit. Asking for help on the toilet is just as effective as sitting in a church building. He still hears you. Just be careful though, as some of the new churches worship the dead. New Age churches seem to neglect the fact that the thanks should be directed to our Creator. Instead, their worship seems to be pointed to the dead humans that they want to hear from.

Try and see it from this point of view. Even the souls in spirit, who have crossed over, know that faith is to be put in Him, not in another human being. All humans are equal, whether living or dead. Those in spirit now come to help their loved ones, as much as they are allowed. They can't solve all your problems for you because you are here to learn and grow. They are simply stopped from sorting everything out, as this would mean that you would never experience the emotional lessons.

Love

This one sounds easy. We all know how to love, but you guys on earth only relate this emotion to a few chosen people in your life. You focus on your family or your romantic partners, but love also needs to be felt for strangers, situations and yourself. Yes that's right, love for yourself. You can't leave yourself out of this one. Remember the lack of self worth we talked about earlier? Right, so try this little exercise just for one day:

Repeat after me – "Thank you for making me, me", just do it – no arguing and after a few days you will see why....

Now think about those words. After a lifetime of looking at and watching other people, you will have realised that you are stuck the way you are.

I bet you can list a whole page worth of things that you don't like about yourself. You were made the way you are, so deal with it. You look the way you look, so deal with that too. You have curly hair, you hate it, but I bet the person with thin ratty straight hair would quite happily commit murder to get some of that bounce from you. Your nose is crooked, oh get a life – look at your beautiful teeth or your finger nails and think how the person next to you would again jump you to have a bit of that.

Now reverse that list and try and write down the things you are lucky and pleased to have

_____

_____

_____

_____

Struggling? Need a hand?
Okay, so now write this list.
My friends' problems that I am glad I don't have:

_____

_____

_____

_____

See how lucky you are?

Instead of looking at other people with envy, today I want you to look at people without the help of the green eyed monster. Even the most beautiful of people struggle with what life has thrown at them.

Try and understand why other people are the way they are. Bent over in the shoulders often shows you that they have reverted inwards because they have been emotionally hurt, or have been excluded in some way, possibly from society.

The ones who look immaculate with their faces painted like a doll, what are they hiding? Bad skin?
Learn to love your body as a channel – it has been given to you for a reason. Remember that.

If you think are not what society now says is beautiful – maybe you need to be different, so that others will warm to you and not be threatened by you. Maybe, just maybe, you are the most attractive human being on the planet, to one person. It's just you who can't see your beauty. That is a priceless knowing.

Honesty

This one sounds simple. Don't lie. That means even white lies – you know the ones where you skirt around the truth. We over here put our heads in our hands when we see lies. They are nearly always told through fear, you realise. Go back to the fear chapter and work on that. What's the worst thing that can happen if you tell the truth? Oh yes, people might think less of you – and your ego wouldn't be able to deal with that, would it?

Start forgiving yourself for doing things wrong. Go on! Be kind to yourself, stop being so damn hard on yourself TODAY. You are not perfect, you make mistakes and this is okay with the big Boss. He still loves ya, so give yourself a break. Do the right thing, apologise to the necessary parties, tell the truth and then move on from it.

However, it's not only about telling porky pies to other people, it's about being honest with yourself. Mmmmm, this is a tricky one. Admitting to yourself that your life is pretty shit at times is hard going, or admitting that you're not proud of your recent actions towards another person, or situation. I am not asking you to do anything about it, yet. I am just asking you to admit to yourself that you are not happy – can we go there today? No? Then re-read this section tomorrow, when you feel a little happier, bud.

When you are ready to discuss this, ask yourself what it is that you are frightened of? People never wanting to talk to you again, or people thinking badly of you? Don't worry about what other people are thinking of you. Just you worry about what you think of yourself. Be proud of who you are – if you are not right now, then change your ways so that you can be.

CHAPTER 2
The Human Chakras

So, we have covered all the ways you can block us from being able to communicate with you. Now let's discuss what damage you can do to your physical body, by not being a pure channel.

You see, your human body is an amazing suit made specifically for you and it is capable of doing so much. It has a lifetime guarantee; all you need to do is look after it properly. You feed it, water it and exercise it, just like you would a pet.

Why is it that so many of you don't do these simple things? Well, go back through the list in the previous chapter; it could be any one of these reasons, such as:

- **Fear**
- **Lack of Self Worth**
- **Ego**
- **Anger**
- **Gains**

You see, every physical illness in your body stems from an emotional problem.

The energy centres in your body control the good health and wellbeing of each part of your body. A negative emotion will stop these centres from spinning healthily and will eventually, if not dealt with, start affecting the wellbeing of the physical organs in that area of your body.

Let's take a look:

The Root Chakra

Seen as the colour red
Located in the groin area

When healthy and working properly, this chakra connects you to the earth's energies. It gives stability in life, patience, courage and success.

When it's not working properly, you will experience uncertainty, low self esteem and lack of confidence.

If left unhealthy for too long, physical problems will start to occur in the pelvis, testes, genitals and legs.

The Navel Chakra

Seen as the colour orange or red-orange
Located just below your belly button

When healthy and working properly, you are full of new ideas, you will have strength and an ability to succeed in life.

Creativity and passion come from this chakra.

When it's blocked, you will become withdrawn, feel lethargic, tired and run down.

If left for too long, the organs that will start to show signs of problems are the ovaries, kidneys, lower stomach, spleen and prostate.

The Solar Plexus Chakra
Seen as the colour yellow
Located in your stomach below your ribs

This chakra, when working properly, ensures that you feel confident and gives you a high self esteem.
This is where you get the gut feeling telling you to do, or not to do something.
A strong healthy solar plexus is needed to develop your psychic skills.
This chakra is also vital for your sense of humour guys.
When this chakra has a problem, you will notice physical problems with the digestive system, liver and gall bladder.

The Heart Chakra
Seen as the colours green and pink
Located in the centre of your chest

This is your love centre and is often the focus of a healing session.
Hurtful situations like divorce, separation, grief and abuse or abandonment, unfaithfulness and betrayal will all affect this chakra deeply.
When it is working properly, you will be able to love and value yourself as well as have wonderful attachments to other human beings.
When it is not functioning properly, it can be a very painful and lonely life, because you will struggle to let others in.
Physical illnesses resulting from this chakra not working properly include heart problems and illnesses affecting the lungs, beginning with bronchitis, and leading onto the dreaded 'C' word.

The Throat Chakra
Seen as the colour blue
Located in the throat

When this chakra is healthy and working properly you are able to express your feelings openly and honestly, communicating with yourself and other people truthfully.
Problems begin with this chakra, when you lie and cannot honestly express how you feel about a situation.
The first sign of a health issue here will be a constant tickle in your throat, soreness leading to laryngitis and other throat problems.
Physical parts of the body affected by this chakra are throat, mouth and the thyroid gland.
Work on honesty and facing your fears to keep this chakra healthy.

The Third Eye Chakra
Seen as the colour Indigo
Located in the forehead

When working properly you are able to develop your intuition, psychic vision and concentration levels.
It is one of the most important chakras to keep healthy if you want to see spirit.
Physical parts of the body that will become affected when this chakra is not healthy include the central nervous system, ears, nose, sinuses and the lower brain.

The Crown Chakra

Seen as the colour white and purple
Located just above the head

When working properly, this chakra connects you to the source of energy that you channel from up above.

Imagine it as a door opening up for the energy to run through you, so you can see why it is vital to keep this one healthy.

When not working properly, it is impossible for spirit to make themselves heard.

You will notice physical problems in the upper brain and pituitary gland.

Remember the colours associated with each chakra because, when working with spirit, particularly when healing others, they will often show you a colour to indicate where you need to focus your attentions, or where the other person's problem truly lies. You may get flashes of a particular colour or you may see swirls of it fill the room, in your mind's eye. Don't be frightened, it is a fantastic way for your guides to communicate with you before you actually hear their voices.

Let me give you a little hint as to how your body screams out what its problem is….. Customers will come dressed in the colour relating to the blocked chakra. Honestly! Their emotional issue even affects the clothes they wear. Try it out – diagnose yourself right now!

Dressed in black from head to toe? Why are you trying to hide yourself? Blues (any shades)? Got an issue with saying how you honestly feel about an area in your life? Greens? There's that old devil called love again – have a battered and bruised old heart, have we?

So you see, your body has the ability to heal itself, if you listen to what it is telling you. It all starts with an emotion. Sort your emotional issues out, and then you won't have any blocks for us to work through.

Next time you are feeling under the weather, run through this list before you call the doc and see if you can diagnose the root of the problem and deal with it, to prevent the 'dis-ease' from getting any worse.

Feeding your body with healthy food is essential. There is one rule. If it grew naturally, without the aid of chemicals and factories, then it is good for you.

Our Creator has supplied you with a complete range of foods that your body needs, not only to use as fuel, but to heal itself with too. Research this for yourself. Your body needs a complete set of vitamins and minerals to function properly; it does not need the ones out of a tub, which were made in a factory, but the ones from fruit and veg. Google 'God's Pharmacy' on the internet – you may be pleasantly surprised.

Anything that involves chemicals, will affect your body's make up. It stops your body from knowing what the hell it is taking in. It confuses the brain, which then doesn't know where to disperse the goodness. The chemicals stay in your body for a very long time, lodging themselves deep inside your tissue and swimming around in your bloodstream causing, sometimes fatal, diseases to start.

Bloody obvious I would have thought. Yet people say they 'doctor' or enhance food to make it look more palatable. So, err a tomato needs to be sprayed with chemicals to make it redder and firmer looking? Oh come on – surely a tomato is a tomato. Oh hang on – or is it really so that the food can sit on the shelf for longer and make money? That's more like it. Shame on society for letting these money grabbing shopkeepers get their way.

Spend some time listening to your body and hearing what it craves. In time, you will be craving random things, like pineapple that you never knew your body even recognised!

You don't need to have an overloaded plate of over cooked food each night – you simply need a variety of fresh natural food to keep healthy. Small regular amounts of raw veg, is a damn sight better than a plate load of mushy food. Think about it!

Why are you being lectured on healthy eating? You wanted to develop your psychic abilities so work with us, so that we can work through you. When channelling properly, you will use all of your body to do so.

CHAPTER 3
Why Do You Want to Channel Spirit?

Ask yourself the above question and be honest.

For recognition?

Then take this book to a charity shop and let it go to a good home.

To be able to channel messages for other people really well?

Start the engine – we are still going to a second hand shop.

For guidance?

Then carry on reading. I'm hoping I can help you.

CHAPTER 4
Guides

Imagine being in spirit world or Heaven yourself. Because once upon a time; you were.

There you were with a whole bunch of people and friends who loved you unconditionally. They were all ready to support you on your impending journey, reassuring you that you would not be alone and they would be right behind you. Those same friends are now called your guides.

They promised you that they would be there, right beside you every step of the way and they have kept that promise. They understand that you might not be able to see them, or hear them once wearing the human 'suit'. However, they have other ways of communicating with you, such as through your gut. You know that gut feeling that churns, or makes you feel excited? You know, when you just know to do something like to turn left instead of right, or to say yes instead of no?

They step in so many times to save your backside, you just don't realise it. Ever had the awful realisation of – if you hadn't delayed leaving work you would have been involved in the motorway pile up, which you just heard about on the news? Or, if you hadn't changed your mind about going out, you would have missed a very important call or visitor?

Give these guys some credit. Even if you can't see them just yet, you are never alone in this life. You may lack other human beings around you at times, but trust me when I say; you have a whole room full of friends, right by your side.

Let's get to know them shall we?

Hopefully, this explains why you hear a lot of people say, when they finally meet their guide, "It feels like I have met a long lost friend", or that it felt like they have known their guide for years.

Your guides have been told not to interfere. They have to patiently wait, just like a parent does with an obnoxious teenager who thinks they know it all....

Sometimes, they never get to show themselves or communicate with you directly, but that doesn't mean that they go away. Even people who are so closed down to the idea of spirit, that they resemble a boarded up building, have guides standing right beside them.

So, you will also hear some people say that their guides are their relations, who have passed over. Eeerrmmmm.... no sorry, that's not the case. Yes, they can give advice, yes, you can channel them, yes, you can have conversations with them, but no, they are not your guides.

This is where a lot of people make mistakes. They channel souls in spirit, not knowing who they are and believe that the advice is good. People seem to think that because the words came from spirit then it must be gospel. Think again!

When your Grandma was alive, was she always right? Or, did she give you the best advice she could think of because she loved you and wanted to help you? Can you think of a time when she wrong, or maybe a time when you didn't actually agree? How about that old conversation, which started with "In my day, we had to walk everywhere, you youngsters don't realise how lucky you are."

Your Grandma is there and yes, you are really able to channel her, but she is not a guide. If you want to be able to chat to her and get the same kind of advice as she would have given when she was alive, then great – go ahead and channel her. However, don't get angry with her when she gets something wrong.

She is just simply giving you her opinion, based on her own human experience and her love for you. You may well stand up as a professional and give advice from her to others, feeling comfortable because you know her like the back of your hand. However, the advice you will be giving out may not necessarily be in that person's best interest.

If you have a problem and you want to phone a friend for advice, you actually choose which friend to call, don't you? You know deep down that Friend A will tell you what you want to hear and sympathise with you. You also know that if you phone Friend B they will tell you what to do, by giving you practical advice. Friend C however, will give you a good talking to and make you aware of the other side of the situation. Depending on what mood you are in and how fragile you are feeling, you will choose a different friend to phone each time.

When you channel a guide, whose job it is to give directional advice, based on that person's path, then you may well be shocked at some of the messages you pass on. You may actually disagree, but when you are channelling properly and faithfully, you will trust.

It is quite funny to see Rhiannon in the zone, channelling my advice to customers quite happily and confidently. Only then, after they have gone, when she is back to the insecure, neurotic woman she has become, she hits the ground running in panic at the thought of what she has just told her customer to do.

So you see, I still battle with her and her trust issues, but she gets the channelling bit right. We just have to work on her, to continue to trust, even when she s not working. Same old, same old – "I am not worthy!" She feels worthy, when the message from me is for other people, but not worthy to receive one for herself. Ring any bells?

It doesn't make any difference who the message is for, the same rule applies. Listen to your guide and your life will become easy and will be a pleasure to live.

So when you get to the stage where you can see and recognise your guide, you may be slightly disappointed about how they appear to you. Mmmmm, can you imagine Rhiannon's horror at discovering I was an Irish dwarf? Not the stereotypical Native American or Spiritual Warrior that she was hoping for, eh?

She wanted to be taken seriously and she got me instead – an all singing, all dancing foul mouthed little dude, but let's see why we were paired up. If you all knew the real Rhiannon, you would know that from childhood, she has had an insane sense of humour and the ability to use it to get her through the darkest hours. On her current path, she needed humour as a tool to survive. So I was sent.

So don't go looking at someone else's guide and think to yourself that you would rather borrow them. You can't just pick another person's guide as your own you know. You may well be able to see them when channelling, but you sure as hell can't make them work with you. That's a bit disrespectful to your own crew, isn't it? They have waited all your life to be able to be seen, by you.

We guides in spirit chuckle. Many people working through egos try and out do one another by declaring they have the most flamboyant, hugely decorated and important guides in history.

Guides show themselves to you in a way that makes you feel comfortable with their presence. They need to build your trust. They may well show themselves from a time, or an era, that you felt most comfortable in, once upon a time. Yes, you have lived here many, many times, my friend. Get over it.

Guides may also show themselves in a way that you simply feel safe with. In truth, if you could see them for what they really are, they would all look like a shining bright white/golden figure, for this is the soul. They don't need a body, being in spirit, but they appear in this way to make you feel at ease.

One golden rule when channelling – say what you see because you see it for a reason.

You are sent as many guides as you need for different areas and times in your life.

Throughout life, more guides will appear to work through you. You have your personal guides to support you and help you grow. If you decide to work to help others and channel messages or healing, then you will have new guides who appear to work through you for each of these.

If you decide to concentrate on channelling to heal physical bodies, you will meet a guide who is just for that purpose. If you progress and want to teach others, you will have new guides who teach through you.

If you just decide to work with spirit and communicate with them on a personal level, then you will have a whole team with you for that too. No difference – you can't escape it, help is at hand, no matter what you decide to do with it. There is help waiting for you in every area of your life on earth.

Whilst you are working you will also see other people in spirit, sometimes they just come to have a little look at what you are doing. Leave them be, you don't need to latch onto them. Focus on what you are doing – acting as a channel for spirit to do their job through you.

Seeing John the Baptist whilst channelling healing one day, Rhiannon became all excited and lost the plot for a moment. I mean to be able to say that you had John the Baptist as a guide, would be really great yeah? No, he is not her guide, but yes, he came to assist. Maybe he was there with the client, or maybe he was just there to help.

Constantly working at being a pure channel and removing all blocks such as ego, is vital. No matter how long you have been doing it and, no matter how professionally you rate yourself, keep working to improve.

Seeing spirit is wonderful and essential, but it doesn't mean you are being guided by all of them. Here, we are talking about guides – in another chapter we will talk about what to do with all the other random peeps you will meet along the way.

When you are completely trusting that spirit are leading the way in your life, you will become aware of how many guides you actually have.

Whilst sitting in a business meeting, Rhiannon became aware that she was taking on a different energy and was able to participate in a conversation that was way over her head. She soon realised that she even had a chap to help her with finances and business decisions. She then noted that every time he appeared, her throat would get blocked and she would feel the need to clear it before the wise words came out of her mouth. To this day, this is her sign that he is around.

She doesn't need to get to know what he looks like, or what his name is, or the grand story that comes with him; she just trusts him and recognises his ways.

The minute she acknowledged that every single aspect of her life was guided and that she really wasn't alone, her life became more bearable. It all comes down to trust again. You really don't have to stress about anything. Just channel.

I am sure you have all heard at least one person say that they can call upon the parking angels. Every time they need a parking space in a hurry, they can order one by asking for it. Funny that – ask for help and you receive the help. Simple really!

So what if you only have one guide? Does that mean you're not as good as the next person channelling? Oh be serious, please! Do you really think you only have one guide? Of course you have more; you just don't need to focus on them all just yet. They don't need to be recognised, they just get on with their job quietly.

With all the different areas of your life, let me guarantee you that there is an army of helpers, right behind you. You just maybe need to focus on one of them, at this present time. Build up a relationship with the one you have, get to know each other and build the trust so that it is water tight and can't be broken by another human. The others will come if and when you are ready.

Even children and babies have guides. Remember your guides are there with you from birth. You, the earth parent, have been trusted, by our Creator, to carry these children on their journey, but imagine it as children sitting in a school classroom. There is a parent, or loved one at home waiting excitedly to see how their child has progressed in the day. That's what their guides do; wait patiently whilst they are in the classroom called Earth.

You may see babies and children talk to themselves as they play with an imaginary friend. Not so imaginary really – none of us are ever alone.

So this brings us onto a deep and hard conversation. Why are people left to suffer in this world, especially babies if they are surrounded by guides to keep them safe? Well, let's not forget that you are all here to learn emotional lessons. You cannot take anything back home with you except for lessons of the heart and the experience you gain whilst on this earth. Each soul has agreed beforehand, what emotional lesson they need to experience this time round.

If you look back at your life, you can probably see a pattern of what your lesson of the heart has been, or is currently. If you started off with a bad childhood – neglect, abuse and loneliness, what is your lesson in love as an adult? Is it the painful – learning to trust? Have you chased love, just wanting to be accepted by other humans? Each one of you chooses, in advance, the life you have on earth. Your guides were sitting with you and agreed to let these lessons happen. They cannot step in and intervene, unless it has been pre-planned or, if you ask them to.

No, the child did not ask to be physically hurt. Remember each human is responsible for their own actions. Parents, in particular, are expected to love and protect their children.

Please note – you can have help with any painful experience, simply by asking for it. The help may not come in the way you expected, but help will definitely come. Your help may come in the form of soulmates, who are sent in the human disguise of new friends, or it may be new guides who will appear to give the required strength or direction. Remember your guides know what emotion you are here to experience.

CHAPTER 5
Getting Started

Every time you channel, you need to make sure you are safe. Who knows what bad boys are lurking around? You don't want to be talking to strangers, now do ya?

Before you begin, light a candle. A simple flame is an easy way of attracting the light in the world. It is a reminder of purity and good intent. It doesn't matter if it is a tea light, or a huge impressive church candle, as long as it's a light.

In a place where you can't use a real flame? No problem, just envisage, imagine, or 'see' a flame in your mind's eye, or a golden ball of bright light in front of you.

Now, you need to make yourself focus on the job in hand. We can't have your mind wandering during this, so we need to ground you.

Sit or stand with your feet firmly on the floor.

Close your eyes.

Imagine or 'see' the roots of an old oak tree growing from the soles of your feet and pushing through into the concrete floor. Push them harder and further down, through the foundations, through the concrete, through the earth. See more and more roots grow, becoming thicker and thicker and longer and longer.

Keep pushing them down and watch them wrap themselves around boulders deep down in the earth, attaching you firmly. Push them harder and watch them reach the centre of the planet.

34

Suddenly, you will see a ball of bright white light shining in the core of the earth – so bright it's almost blinding. Begin to breathe in deeply and with each breath, you are drawing up the light through the roots.

Keep breathing calmly until you see the light travel right up to the soles of your feet, filling each and every root that you are attached to.

Another slow, deep breath and the light zooms up your legs, filling every blood vessel and muscle. Your legs and feet will begin to feel nice and warm. They may also feel like concrete blocks.

Keep breathing and drawing up the light until your entire body is filled. See it. Feel it fill your thighs, your torso, travelling up your spinal cord, spreading out to fill the sides of your body and every muscle.

It now fills your ribs, your lungs and your neck and down your arms, all the way to your finger tips. Your hands and fingers may feel tingly now, wiggle them and let the energy flow inside you.

See the light fill your head entering every single brain cell and finally, it pours out of the top of your head through the crown chakra, forcing it open.

See the light cascading down around the side of your body like a waterfall. It's never ending – all you have to do, to have another surge, is breathe in deeply.

Now open your eyes and study how you feel. Do your feet feel heavy? Does your body feel hot and pain free?

No? Do it again, with passion and see everything I have explained.

Yes? Excellent – proceed to the next step.

Now, we need to protect you.

This is so simple, but essential. Imagine or 'see' in your mind's eye a clear bubble around the whole of you. Sit yourself inside it. Like a hamster ball or a washing up bubble. You can see through it. You can breathe in it. This is a bubble of protection and it prevents you from picking up on other peoples' feelings and emotions.

Hey, you are here to help others and sympathise with them and even feel their pain, so you can diagnose and prove that you are connected to them, but you sure as hell don't need to take on their problems. If you don't bubble and protect yourself whilst working, don't come running and complaining that you're feeling drained and exhausted. Your client will feel just great after seeing you, but you will be left ruined. The idea is that you are able to help them, understand what they are going through, sympathise even, but not take on their problems, be it physical or emotional.

Now when you are working with your guides, you will find that people are automatically drawn to you. People will come and ask you for advice; they will appear in your life randomly, asking if you can help them. It's a bit like you are walking around with a sign on your head that says "I can help you". So, if you get caught unawares or off guard, you will be glad you grounded and protected when you woke up in the morning.

Do this in preparation for meeting a client and at any time you are about to tune in to work with spirit.

You are also protecting yourself from souls in spirit. There are good guys and not so good guys, over here. Would you stop and talk to just anyone in the street if you felt threatened, or if they looked a little unsavoury? Of course you wouldn't. Lets smash out the idea that just because they are dead, it's okay to speak to them right now. When you die and leave your body, your personality, your soul's make up, stays the same. So, if you were a lovely genuine, caring person who smiled a lot and was a kind hearted person, you will still come across like that, from over here. If you were an angry, impatient, unsociable or an overpowering kind of person, you will still come across like that too. You, as a channel, feel and take on the personality and energy of the soul.

So would you feel comfortable with talking to someone like that who was alive? Would you let them into your house for coffee? No, so why on earth you guys think it's okay to do so when they are dead, I will never understand. You need to go back to the ego check, in the earlier chapter and ask yourself why you are doing this for a job. You must not forget that 'working with spirit' does not have to be unpleasant; you do not have to suffer and feel fear at any point. That's not what your guides want you to experience.

You have to start at the beginning – building up experience and confidence. This could take years. If you are all about ghost busting and feeling the fearsome dudes from day one, then please stop reading now. You're scaring me!

Now if you are asked, by spirit, to help the troubled dead, then that's a different story. Refer to the relevant chapter, later on in the book, where I talk about rescue work.

The most important thing that I have to tell you is how to close down. So many people don't do this and it is vital to keep you safe and healthy. If you don't, you will be walking around for the rest of the day channelling everyone and anyone in spirit and you will become drained. It is irresponsible of you to allow this. Your batteries will get worn out very quickly and you will no longer be protected. Well, don't blame us, when you have a nasty experience with someone, on the other side.

So when you have finished channelling or working with spirit and you are ready to go about your normal private life routine, close down. To do this simply close the crown chakra that you saw bursting open with the golden light flowing out and cut the roots from under your feet. Keep the bubble of protection around you – even put a new one around you, if you like. Sometimes it's hard to visualise the crown chakra closing, so imagine or 'see' a trap door being closed in your scalp. Bang it down with a few nails and a hammer in your mind's eye, if you must. Just do whatever it takes, to tell yourself mentally that you have closed down and have finished channelling for the present moment in time.

If you don't close down, how will you get on with the rest of your day? How will you give your children, spouses, or friends your attention? How will you focus on doing the grocery shopping, if you are still being badgered by spirit? Do not be afraid to tell us that you are busy and that now is not the time to set you to work. If you walk around open and ready to channel at every given moment, then we will assume you are okay with this. Don't blame your guide when your marriage packs up and your children start saying you don't seem to care about them anymore.

As with other people in your life – such as the dreaded mother in law, there is a time and a place for people coming to visit. This includes us, okay?

So we have grounded and protected. Now follow some simple exercises to help you start to see and hear your guide.

Meditation

I know in your busy 100mph lives, it is hard to find time to be able to sit still, but please try at least once a week. It will benefit you greatly. In time, this simple meditation will help you to meet your guide and give you a private space to be able to chat with him or her.

If at first you don't see anyone, then just be. That means sit still, enjoy the peace and make note of how you feel physically and emotionally. You see, I guarantee your guide is there, it's your end that is preventing you from seeing them. Go back through the list of potential blocks and start the meditation process again.

Don't worry – they can wait, they are not going anywhere.

Read the following meditation through, until you are familiar with it, then put the book down and walk yourself through it.

Imagine yourself sitting down in the middle of a beautiful empty field.

Put your hands down and feel the blades of grass all around you. Kick your shoes off and let the blades of grass touch your feet. Lie down with your knees bent, so your feet are firmly on the grass and your arms are flat down beside you.

There's a beautiful blue sky, with a few white puffy clouds. As you close your eyes you can feel the warmth of the sunshine on your face.

Relax yourself, enjoy the peace. When you're ready, see yourself sit up and look around.

To your right, is a small gate leading out of the field. Through it you can see a path beside a gentle stream.

When you're ready, stand up and walk slowly towards the gate. Hear the birds singing, feel the sunshine and breathe in deeply and calmly as you walk across the field.

You're now leaning on the gate, looking down the path. On the left hand side, is a beautiful big oak tree, the leaves are green and you can hear the gentle breeze rustling through them.

On the right hand side of the path, you can see the stream and hear the water gently running over the pebbles.

When you're ready, open the gate and stand on the shingled path. As you take steps slowly along the path, look down and become aware of the tiny beautiful red flowers growing along the side. Stop. Bend down and pick one. Study the colour and the delicateness of the petals.

Continue on the path, taking in all the beautiful scenery as you go.

Look down again, on the right hand side of the path, on the grass verge is a cluster of flowers growing wildly. This time, the petals are bright orange. Choose which one you want to take with you.

Continue on slowly and calmly, the birds are still singing. Become aware of the gentle wildlife that can be heard, all around you. Know you are safe and are in a peaceful place.

A few more steps along the path and on the right hand side, on the grass verge, more flowers can be found. This time there are beautiful yellow petals on the tiniest, yet most perfect flowers. Pick one and add it to your collection.

Continue on down the path and soon you will become aware of a beautiful green bush filling the verge. The lush green leaves surround beautiful delicate pink flowers. Pick a flower and one of the green leaves and add them to your collection.

A few steps along the path, the tiniest of blue flowers can be seen growing wildly along the grass verge. Pick on and carry on with your journey.

Study all of the flowers in your hand and see all the bright colours as rays of light. Feel the warmth that comes through your body.

Now you stand still on the path looking forward and you can see a beautiful, wooden arched bridge that is leading to the other side of the stream. At the foot of the bridge, there are the most beautiful indigo coloured long stemmed flowers. Pick the prettiest, brightest one you can find and add it to your collection.

Stand at the beginning of the bridge and steady yourself by holding onto the side and prepare yourself to step onto it. As you look across, you see the brightest of white lights, cascading along the bridge to meet you.

In a minute, when you're ready, you are going to cross the bridge and enter the white light. You are completely safe, relaxed and at ease. If you do not feel ready to cross the bridge, sit down and just enjoy the peace and feeling of tranquillity.

If you are ready to cross the bridge, do so now. On the other side, there is a bench, right at the entrance to the greenest, lushest woods. Sit on the bench with your collection of flowers and wait to be greeted by your guide.

You may hear, you may see, you may feel, or you may experience nothing at all, except for peace. If you do see, or hear your guide, enjoy the conversation and enjoy the experience. Do not be afraid to ask questions, but take the answers that you're given.

Stay seated on the bench, for at least 10 minutes and when you are ready to leave, it is vital that you retrace your steps to come back down to earth. So when you're ready to return, say "Thank you" and "Goodbye", to your guide.

Leave the flowers on the bench and start to slowly make your way back over the bridge. Turn left and feel the small stones of the path on the soles of your feet. Now the stream is on your left and the huge oak tree is on your right.

You are feeling happy, content, relaxed and inspired. Proceed to the gate that takes you into the field.

Walk through the gate making sure you close it firmly behind you. Return to the same spot where you were lying in the field. Lie back down, touch the grass with your hands, feel the sun shining on your face and become aware of your surroundings. When you're ready, open your eyes and notice the surface you are on.

Repeat this meditation as often as you like. Taking yourself off, to your private space over the bridge, is priceless. Don't be afraid if you travel off to a different location either – know that you are safe at all times. This is an opportunity for your guide to show you what they need you to see. If, at anytime, you feel uncomfortable – leave. Retrace your steps and start all over again, making sure the roots are strong and secure from the soles of your feet.

Fell asleep? That's fine, but don't do this meditation in bed at night time. I can't stress how important it is to bring yourself back down to earth.

So what did you see? What did you feel, when you successfully saw someone at the bench?

Accept what you saw, take it and say "Thank you", in your mind.

We have lift off!

Maybe you only felt a presence; maybe you only saw your surroundings and not a person. That's fine for starters. Your guide will come when he or she knows that you can handle it. They know when you are ready, more so than you do yourself.

Rhiannon screamed at us lot a few years ago, demanding to be able to see spirit. We told her she wasn't ready. She argued, saying "Yes, I am!" out loud, like the diva she thought she was. We soon shut her up by flashing 6ft images of people in front of her. She nearly fell over backwards and begged us to stop. We proved she wasn't ready. It took her weeks to calm down and stop looking over her shoulder.

CHAPTER 6
Learning to Work Together

Talk to them. KNOW that they are there with you. KNOW that they are walking on the right hand side of you.

We are working so hard from this side to help you to open. For us it's like tuning in a radio to the right station. We have to tune you into the right frequency, before we can work through you.

A great little tool to get you communicating with us is a pendulum or dowser. These days, it's normally a crystal on a chain – there are loads to choose from and they are easy to stick in your pocket.

Hold the end of the chain gently draped over the side of your fore finger and secured with your thumb. Hover it over the palm of your other hand, a good few inches up so it doesn't touch your skin.

Now imagine your guide standing behind you. Ask them clearly in your head or out loud, "Please show me – yes". The dowser will begin to turn gently in a circle. Note which way it turns, either clockwise or anti-clockwise.

If it does not move, then you are not asking your guide with true intent. Maybe you do not believe me, or maybe you feel slightly stupid. Let's try again.... Trust me, this is working with your energy and, it is really is your guide communicating yes/no answers with you.

Now, ask the question, "Please show me – no." The dowser will now turn in the opposite direction to the yes answer.

Now, one more time, this time asking the question, "Please show me – I don't know." It will move yet again, but now in a different direction – usually up and down forcefully.

Practise this as many times as needed until you are confident about how your guide is answering you using your new toy.

Please note that if you give your dowser to a friend to play with, it may well turn in different ways. This is because it's their guide working with them and not yours.

Also, each and every time you go to use it, ask the same three questions first, before you start working with it. This is because it could very well be a different guide talking to you the next time you pick it up. So, always clarify the way they answer you, first.

Now you and your guide can begin to have fun. You can ask them anything that can be answered with a yes, no, or don't know answer. Try it – have fun.

It's fantastic for finding things that you have lost. Go into each room and ask is the missing item in the room and your guide will soon re-unite you with the object

A lot of people begin to smell spirit first. You may get a waft of aftershave, or perfume, or a cooking smell. Acknowledge whatever you are given and work with it. You will soon recognise that the same smell comes to you each time you attempt to talk to your guide. Same as when you connect with a friend, or relative in spirit, which is easier as you will already recognise your Grandma's perfume, or the smell of tobacco from your Granddad. Just accept whatever smell you are given as a sign.

Remember TRUST.

Just simply thinking of a person who has passed over will bring them close to you. Acknowledge any faintest smell you get. The more you acknowledge it and do not dismiss it, the more you will be able to smell in the future.

Your loved ones and your guides are afraid of scaring the hell out of you and making you shut down instantly through fear. Sending a familiar smell is a good gentle way for all concerned to start communications off.

So, a sense of smell is usually first, then comes the hearing, followed by the actual seeing.

Don't be alarmed if you suddenly hear a voice calling your name, or become aware of a conversation when you are alone. It starts off with background noise and you will turn around to see where it's coming from. It's just us tuning you in. You are not using your human ears, on the side of your head for this. This is all coming from your third eye chakra, located in the centre of your forehead.

It may actually help, to begin with, if you cover your ears with your hands. See if you can still hear the background noise and zone into it. They may not be talking to you directly, but just practise being able to hear them. It's a bit like putting a glass up to your neighbour's wall, to listen in on their argument.

Another good way to develop your ability to hear us is to try tuning in just before going to sleep. A few minutes before you fall asleep, is the time when your physical body is at its most open and relaxed. This is simply because the controlling side of your brain is shutting down.

Whilst lying down flat on your back in bed with your legs uncrossed and your arms down by your side, see the golden light from above shoot down directly through your stomach and fill your body entirely. Feel the warmth inside you, know you are safe.

Still your mind and feel your body begin to get heavy. Your ears will ring, don't be afraid, just go with it. Suddenly, you will hear a conversation start. Just listen, you probably won't be able to make sense of what you hear, which is okay. You've stepped into it mid conversation.

No doubt you will freak and close down through fear the first time. Try not to. Start all over again with the golden light and know you are safe.

Just listen to the voices. Accept what you hear and with practise you will soon be able to chat together.

When you have experienced this a few times, I want you to try this next stage. In your mind ask a question that you know the answer to, such as, "How many children do I have?" Then answer yourself in your mind.

You heard the answer after the question was asked, right? Now ask another question that you know the answer to and another and another. When it is you answering yourself, the answer will always come after the question has been asked. When it is spirit talking to you, the answer will come, still in your own voice, but before you have finished asking the question.

Try it and see.

Test us. Use questions that you know the answer to. The voice will sound like your own, but don't be put off thinking you're doing it wrong. When the answer comes into your mind, half way through you asking the question, you know you have made contact.

Now try it in the daytime, whilst walking around doing everyday chores. Ask the question. Dismiss your own answers after a pause and only accept the ones that come instantly. This is huge progress my friend.

Now up the stakes and ask questions that you don't know the answer to. Again, don't be afraid to test us. For example, "Will I hear from a long lost friend today?" or "Will I get a phone call from XXXX today?"

It's important to remember that we have no sense of time here in spirit, like you do on earth, so always state when your challenge is up. Otherwise you may well get the call tomorrow and declare that your guide got it wrong.

Your guide will never be wrong, but you may have to practise at making yourself understood. Stick with questions that can be answered simply, with "Yes" or "No", to begin with too. Then wait for your proof.

In time, you can up the stakes by asking harder more detailed questions. Your guide really will enjoy the interaction with you and will not mind being tested.

You could try this one, like Rhiannon did with me.

"Okay, if you're real and I'm not going mad, the phone will ring right now."

Yes the phone rang and it was a wrong number just to make her laugh. We can do anything that you want us to do here. You just have to ask, but be specific.

Let's just quickly talk about abusing this friendship.

Do not even think about asking your guide questions to gain materialistically, or to be able to hurt other people. You will not get an answer, or more than likely, if they are anything like me, you will get an answer that will make you look like a fool, the moment you repeat it. Just to ensure your ego, or greed, does not step in.

Betting results? Rhiannon is now cringing typing this one for me.

Years ago, when Rhiannon was eagerly practising, at any given opportunity, she was sitting in bed with her husband, one Sunday morning.

She was shown as clear as anything a grid of football teams, all neatly paired up with a golden winner at the top. Excitedly repeating what she was being shown, to her football loving husband, he grabbed a pen and paper and asked her to slowly and carefully repeat exactly, to the letter, what she saw. Unbeknown to Rhiannon, the World Cup was coming up in a few months time.

Dave went skipping off to the pub that lunchtime with his wife's predictions in hand and announced it to all his fellow drinkers. They rubbed their hands together with glee and all placed bets on the winning team at the top.

Needless to say, they were all completely and utterly wrong.

Dave was furious and Rhiannon thankfully saw the lesson she had learned and took it very gracefully. Had she grounded? Had she protected? Had she opened up to begin work? No! She was unprotected, sitting up in bed, drinking tea and channelling anyone in spirit, who was passing by.

Lesson learned - the hard way.

If she had been open to working properly and professionally, she would not have had an answer at all. You see, we know what you are going to do with the information, even before you do. The information given to you is given for a good reason.

Another example is in a famous missing child case. Rhiannon was desperate to help, not for recognition, but because, as a new mother herself, this had really affected her. She begged to be told where the child was and what had happened to her. We did not answer. She begged some more and even got angry with us. We simply answered her with this, "You cannot handle what has happened." She argued some more. We stayed silent.

Later that day, when we did share a snippet of information, she realised that we were right. She was not emotionally strong enough to have the images, or information given to her. It was too close to home, especially with her new baby in her arms. Plus, would she have been able to cope with the reality of what would have happened, if she did pass on the correct details? Being thrown into the limelight and questioned about her involvement, knowing such detail? No, Rhiannon would, under no circumstances, have been able to deal with any of the consequences. It's not her path, or her job. Leave it to others, who are stronger and more able to remove emotion from the job.

So now you are beginning to talk to your guide, even though you can't yet see them. Get to know each other. Ask questions about him or her, as you would a new best friend. Sit and chat about their opinions on different subjects. Keep notes of the thoughts that come to you. Get to understand and feel their personality. They may be funny, they may be serious. Each time you channel them, you will take on their personality as you are working. Don't worry, you will return back to your joyous self when closed down, but do take time to understand your guide's way of thinking, their sense of humour, etc. You are representing them when channelling their words to the world. You are their voice.

I know Rhiannon gets quite embarrassed at saying some of the things I tell her to say, but the trust and faith she has in me, ensures she never twists or changes my words.

You will also get signs throughout the day. These are answers to your questions. Sometimes Rhiannon is so stubborn and closed down, when she is wrapped up in her grief, that we have to use blimin' great artic lorries, with slogans on the side, to get the answers to her questions across to her.

Her husband, here with us in spirit, is now a dab hand at arranging for a black Volvo to appear in front of her and show the way when she is lost. She screams out loud asking for help and directions, but she doesn't listen to the answers, so now she knows to follow the car in front, when it appears.

The 'thoughts' that pop into your head are easily dismissed. Please take the first thing that is given to you. Don't ponder on it, or wonder if you 'heard' it right. Take the first thing that came into your mind and say it out loud. Even if it is a single word that doesn't make sense to you just yet, trust me when I say "It is right!"

Repeating the word out loud, is clarifying the fact that you are channelling through your head and passing it out through your mouth. All good practise for when you will, very soon, be giving full-on messages to others.

You can practise on willing friends too, but only with their permission please. Tell them what you are doing and why you would appreciate their help.

Now this is where trust really needs to kick in. If you are not careful, your fear of sounding like a total idiot by giving out just a one word message, which means nothing to you, is going to take over. Trust in your guide! He or she will not fail you. Remember the golden rule – say what you get. Don't think about it, ponder on it, change it, dismiss it, or question it. Just say it.

You see, the message is not for you. You are now being asked to pass it on to your friend, the guinea pig. Maybe, just maybe, a family member who has passed away sorted out a code word that they would use if life after death really did exist. Or maybe, just maybe, the word that comes out of your mouth is totally relevant to your friend from a few hours ago. Pass the message on and let your friend explain if it means anything. If it doesn't – don't worry. I guarantee you that your guide is right and they just need to get over their excitement, before they realise what it means.

Next stage is to become aware of how you feel physically when giving this message. Do you feel happy, sad, excited, tired or emotional? Tell your friend what you feel. More often than not, you will be picking up on their emotional state, or even the emotional state of a loved one, who has passed over.

Do not try and understand why you feel like this. This is the control freak side of human nature getting in the way of being a pure channel.

Whoa! How did we get to channelling loved ones rather than our guides???? Your guide is your protector; he or she will be allowing other souls in spirit to pass on messages through you too. Chill and go with the flow.

Always thank your guide, every time you connect.

This is the beginning of a beautiful friendship and a new way of life for you. You have met the one person who will be there for you through thick and thin. Even when you're not being very nice to the outside world, they will still be there for you. This is unconditional love. Basically, you are stuck with each other. This is the person you can trust with your life.

To be able to see your guide, you will have to do a lot of work from the fear chapter, at the beginning of the book. No matter how excited you are at being able to see spirit, it can still be quite a shock when you actually do. Like I said before, your guide will know when the time is right, even before you do. I don't just mean fear of the unknown, as in – being scared. I mean fear of moving forward with this work, fear of getting it wrong, or fear of failure.

Very often, you guys will see us, then have a mini fit and the image will disappear. You tell yourself that we only flashed passed, but the reality is that you cut the connection.

The first thing you do when confronted with a spirit, is to turn around to look more closely. Why? Because when you see us, you are not using your human eyes, you are using your third eye chakra, remember?

When you do manage to see us for the first time, I bet you that it is out of the corner of your eye when you're actually concentrating on something else. When this happens, KEEP looking in the direction that you were – do NOT turn your head. This way, you will not lose sight of us.

Calm yourself and again, make sure you are grounded, protected and ready to channel. After doing this, if what you saw was your guide, or a soul that is safe for you to channel, you will still be able to see and communicate with them. If they have disappeared, in the thirty seconds it took you to ground and protect yourself, say a big "Thank you", to your guide for keeping you safe. That soul was not safe for you to channel.

Now, here are a few exercises to help you develop this ability.

As silly as it may sound, close your eyes. The best clairvoyants are blind people you know – because they are forced to use their third eye and not their human eyes.

It's time to embarrass Rhiannon again. Did you know that when she first started off doing sessions for people privately, she sat there with her hands over her eyes looking like a right idiot?

Now, you try it in private. Shut your eyes and notice what you see. Don't say black, or nothing. Look closer and focus. Now watch tiny spots of white or grey appear. Focus your attention on the tiniest bit of movement in one of those specks. Strobes or flashes of light will appear too, move your eyes around to watch what they do and where they go. The specks of colour will begin to get bigger and maybe you can now see shadows in different shapes. Go with it and watch the darkness disappear and be replaced with patterns and clouds of light.

Now focus your attentions on one particular shape. Watch it turn into something and become aware of what words or thoughts are going through your brain. Soon, the swirl will take the shape of an item or a person. Maybe you can see the outline of a face, or a household item. Whatever it is, accept it. All we are doing here is strengthening your third eye and training you to literally 'see' with it. You will now be combining the hearing and thought processes, with the sight, all essential to be able to see, hear and communicate with spirit properly.

Keep practising this as often as possible. After a while, you will be able to search around in the dark room of your closed eyes and see more stories and events evolve in front of you.

An alternative exercise for you to try is to blur your vision.

Ground, protect and open up.

Squint your eyes and relax them, almost to the point where everything seems blurred. Focus on one object, straight ahead, on the other side of the room and relax your eyes even more. Without turning your head, see how far to both sides you can actually see.

Can you see your hair on the side of your head, or the walls of the room to the left or to the right of you? Isn't it amazing that you can almost see 180 degrees without taking your eyes off the centre of your attention?

Become aware of everything around you in detail. Within time, you will become aware of a shadow or figure just outside of your range. Whilst keeping your eyes on the spot in front of you, focus your attention on this figure.

Describe, to yourself, what you see, hear and feel and ask for confirmation. If you feel confident enough, ask for their name.

Always say "Thank you", when you've finished.

You will also find that your guide will communicate with you whilst you sleep. Your dreams will become more vivid and detailed. You will remember key parts of the dream and realise that they were messages and instructions to better your life. Some dreams are warnings and predictions. Some dreams are an opportunity for you to learn, even whilst you are asleep.

It is a good idea to keep a dream book by the side of your bed, handy for times when you wake up in the middle of the night. Writing down the key points in your dreams is a wonderful way of remembering how your guide likes to communicate with you. Symbols in dreams are often the same as those used by your guide, when passing on a message for a client. So, a good dream dictionary is a great investment.

Whatever you learn – your guide learns too. So, if your dream dictionary tells you that a spider is a sign of money coming to you – then your guide will also show you a spider as a quick sign of money coming. After a detailed in-depth dream that has lasted for hours, you may well only remember the creepy spider running around for a split second, that's because it was, in fact, the most important message in your dream.

Creative writing is another great way of learning to work with your guide. Get a blank piece of paper and have a pen poised. Clear your mind and connect with your guide, as usual.

Become the channel that we need you to be, by clearing all emotional blocks out of the way. Ground, protect and open up. I hope that by now you are feeling your scalp buzz or tingle whenever you connect to the energy through your crown chakra.

Begin writing. Don't try and make sense of it and don't try and write in perfect sentences. In fact, don't even look at the paper, whilst you are writing. At first what you write down will be complete twaddle. The words won't be in the right order, but the trick is to not take the pen off the paper. Join it all up, word after word after word, until you are writing without thinking. Don't stop to look or to check if it makes sense – just keep the flow going.

With technology today, creative writing is easier. Type on a keyboard as you are hearing the words. This is exactly how this entire book was written for me – with Rhiannon typing what she heard me say.

It takes practise and a hell of a lot of trust, to be able to write what you hear and not what you want to hear. Keep at it and then you will have a wonderful record of your conversations with your guide.

You can even type the questions as you ask them in your head, followed by the channelled responses. Go back weeks later and see if what you asked was correctly answered. Remember – we really don't mind you testing us, if it will all lead to us working together, in harmony.

Don't forget to close down when you have finished.

CHAPTER 7
Different Ways of Working with Your Guides

You, I am afraid, are not in control of this one. You were once, that was on the day you agreed to undertake the current path you are on. That was when you and your guides all sat down and discussed what lessons you needed to learn and agreed what work you were to come down to earth to complete. You also agreed who, in spirit, would be available to work with you and, at what time in your life, your guides would step in to assist and carry you through the tough bits.

I have heard many people say "I tried that working with spirit stuff and my life started to go horribly wrong, so I jacked it in fast". Mmmmm, okay, yes life does appear to get harder as you openly let spirit work through you. The lessons do appear to get tougher, but think of it this way – if you don't progress this time round, you'll only have to come round again and do it all over from scratch next time. So, why not get it over and done with now?

You see, the end goal is to learn about all emotions in the human life. Then you become complete and then you get to stay in the Eternal Kingdom – a permanent holiday and rest time. How cool is that?

So what lesson are you here to learn? Loads, my friend! Look back at your life and see the lessons that have been given to you already. Remember, life only gets better when you get the gist of it and then, you can move on.

How about if all of your relationships have gone horribly wrong, everybody has left you and hurt you. You have tried to change to keep another person happy and loving you, but they still left anyway. Then one day, something snaps in you and you say to yourself, "Sod it, I am who I am and if they don't like me, then I am better of on my own." Bingo! Self respect and self worth have been learned. Within a short while, you find that a beautiful soul will walk into your life and accept you, warts and all.

Another thing for you to consider is how can you possibly understand and be sympathetic towards the people that you are asked to help, in this life, if you haven't experienced their path? So, yes, life does get harder and the lessons get bigger when you have signed up to help others. You will be given situations that are painful, in order that you can be a compassionate help to all the people you meet.

Some of You Are Here to Teach Others

Easy to spot – they often have their hardest of lessons to learn in early life, before they can pass on what they have learned. There is nothing worse than a young mother teaching you how to suck eggs, is there? Well, they are all old souls and even they can't understand why they 'know' things. It's because they have learned lessons during their previous times on earth.

No, they are not perfect, it's just that they have been around the track once or twice before. They are no better than you, who are here to learn; in fact these old souls are still learning themselves, to a degree. Quite often though, these people will teach through their hardship and become an inspiration to others. There is nothing to envy here guys, because they have had to live through their sermon.

Let's look at how the times are changing. Fifty years ago, spirit was working hard and furiously through human channels, to prove that life continued on in another realm after death on earth. They did this by using some fantastic mediums that were able to connect with loved ones. The messages were always personal, proving that 'Uncle

Bill' or 'Auntie Flo' could be seen and contacted and that they were watching their loved ones.

These mediums had to work really hard, under lots of criticism. They came under fire from other religious groups, but they successfully managed to get the idea accepted widely. Say a big thank you to this generation of hard working channels as they have made it easier for you today.

Times are changing now and it's time for messages to be given differently.

Rhiannon and I have been asked to work in the new way. I don't want to waste time proving to you that Rhiannon can see Uncle Bill, or the green stripy pyjamas that he used to sleep in. Instead, I want to help you better your life (so does Uncle Bill) and we want to do it by showing you what's coming up in your life and advising you which way to turn for the best. The whole reason for this is that, as a channel, you can help someone see, that by working with spirit and listening to their advice, life on earth becomes a lot easier and more enjoyable.

One particular guy on your TV's has coined a catchphrase that sums it up perfectly – "Bringing the two worlds closer together". If everyone worked with spirit, on a daily basis, life would indeed be great.

Hmmm, so the idea is to also teach others how to do this for themselves? Won't that put you out of a job and make you just one of many? Oh no, you won't be different, unique and special.

Go right back to the ego check and ask yourself, why you are doing this for a job? Remember it's your duty to pass on the message to 'help' people; you're not doing it to look good, or to make yourself big and clever. You are being the voice for your team. Remember that a good teacher creates students, who are better than themselves.

So, how do you feel about the idea of standing up in front of 50 people and throwing out predictions for the future? Passing on messages that no one can praise you for, as they don't know if it's right or wrong yet? Well, it comes down to trust and faith and utter belief in your guides again, doesn't it?

Sometimes, trust me, you may not want to be the bearer of some of the news, such as telling someone that the job they are about to take is not going to work out. However, also being able to tell them that there is another job coming along 3 days afterwards, will be the best part of the message. This is the bit that they will hold onto and remember and so they won't become distraught in their life.

Rhiannon is now used to leaving such evenings with her head held high, but trust me it rocked her at the start. It is always good for the ego to have people come up and say how right the message was, so you can go home feeling good about your job. Be warned – the modern way of giving messages of encouragement and direction, is not for the faint hearted.

You see the problem is that people only hear what they want to hear. You have got to be brave to pass on a message that tells someone to change their job and to detail how and when they are going to get the new one, when all they came to hear about is when they will find love. It's not for you to decide what message spirit have to give them, but then again, spirit already know what they yearn for. Maybe, just maybe, if they listen to the whole message given, they will hear that by changing their job, they will be in the right place to meet their soulmate.

We understand that for you, as the channel, it is hard not to be put off. It is tempting to answer only what the client wants to know, instead of sticking to the job and passing on the message that spirit has given – word for word.

As a result, it's always nice to have feedback and confirmation and, trust me when I say that no matter how long you have to wait, we will get the feedback to you. We want you to continue and will do whatever it takes to keep you working well. So, if you need a pat on the back, we will deliver it at the right time and in the right way, without feeding your ego!

Some of You Are Here to Pass on Healing

You do this so that others can get better and can progress with their own life purpose. Rhiannon has written a neat little book about healing, called "To all Healers, with love from a Healer".

For that book she channelled another dude, who she works with to give healing. It's not my job to heal through her; I just use her to pass messages on. However, physically healing another person's body is done in the same way – by channelling the energy from up above and repairing the damage, which that person has done to themselves, by holding onto fears and emotions. You can also heal a broken body after an accident by passing on the energy, to speed up the natural healing process. Yep, you can fix the damage done to a body, even the big bad boy – cancer.

But what if they don't change their ways? What if they hold onto the same emotional problems? Well …. it comes back! There is a saying that fits this call of duty – "You can only help someone, who wants to be helped". It is indeed heartbreaking to watch the desperation in a person's eyes, when diagnosed with a serious ailment. It is heartbreaking to see that they call a healer only as a last resort, when technology can no longer help and, it is gut wrenching to see, when their fear is so thick, that they go back to their damaging ways instantly. They have used God only as a quick fix.

It is a wonderful feeling though, when people listen to the words coming out of Rhiannon's mouth for real, when she explains that faith and love, for oneself, can conquer all. It is a wonderful feeling, to see the client change their entire way of living, after the healing and, forever.

No names mentioned but here is a heartbreaking example, which left Rhiannon and her daughter scarred for years.

One Friday a phone call came from an extremely distressed pregnant lady. She was asking for help, as her unborn baby had been diagnosed with heart problems. The hospital scan at 20 weeks showed that the heart was back to front; had a hole in one of the tubes and also a hole in the centre of the heart itself. The diagnosis was not good and the lady had been told that she had to go to the specialist team in another hospital, first thing on Monday morning. The mother was so upset and said that she was desperate for Rhiannon to help, as she didn't know what else to do, for the sake of her baby.

Rhiannon cancelled clients who were booked in for readings and told the lady to make her way to the shop instantly, where she and her daughter Hannah, would be waiting to help.

After settling the lady down on the couch, Hannah began to channel the Holy Spirit through the lady's head, whilst Rhiannon put her hands on the bump and prayed. She prayed to be used as a channel and prayed for her personal attachment and emotions to be taken away, so she could do her job properly. She also prayed that she could be allowed to 'see' what was happening.

The baby was distressed, the bump was moving furiously, so Rhiannon spent some time just calming the baby down, passing the energy through her hands. She could see, in her mind's eye, a beautiful blonde girl, with a mass of hair and she passed this on to the mother. It had been confirmed, that morning at the hospital that it was definitely a girl, so this gave the mother confidence that Rhiannon could well help.

Listening to her guide's instructions, Rhiannon moved her hand over the area of the baby's heart and allowed the energy to flow as she watched her guide work through her. Giving a running commentary the whole time, in her usual manner, she described what she was allowed to see.

She watched in awe as her guide took the baby's heart in his hands and massaged gently. She could also feel the softness of organ brush against her hand. She had tears in her eyes, as she was watching surgery being performed on the tubes and she carried on giving the running commentary to the mother. Hannah could see everything too and was just as mesmerised and glued to the spot. Neither of them had ever seen spirit work in such detail before. The mother could feel pain in her stomach and Rhiannon promised her that she was safe and in good hands, with Dr C.

After about half an hour, everything stopped and Rhiannon said that it had finished. The mother was so grateful and all three women began to cry, so blown away were they, with what had just happened. Coming back to just being a simple human being, Rhiannon said she couldn't promise everything was okay, but she sure as hell knew, after that experience that something had been done. She told the mother to go home and rest and phone her with the specialist's results on Monday.

The mother asked how much she should pay, but Rhiannon refused. No way on earth could Rhiannon charge for something like this – she knew spirit would reward her, in other ways, for doing her duty.

Rhiannon and Hannah were wiped out after the lady had gone. They had to close the shop and go home early. They were incapable of pulling themselves together emotionally and were physically drained too, after the whole experience. Rhiannon went home and sobbed, telling her husband how damn lucky they were to have so many healthy children. She worried all weekend and couldn't think of anyone, or anything else, apart from the baby and that poor mother.

Monday morning and, whilst driving in the car, she got a call. It was the mother and her husband screaming down the phone with joy and shock. They had been to the hospital and had another scan. The doctors asked them to explain exactly why the other hospital had sent them, as there was nothing to see except for a healthy baby girl bouncing around. There was no problem with the heart at all and they couldn't understand it.

Rhiannon nearly crashed the car and had to pull over quickly. She laughed and said "Thank you" to spirit, over and over, still in complete shock. When she had calmed herself down, she told the mother to still take it easy and go home and rest. She said she would give her a call to organise another session, in a few days.

About an hour later, whilst Rhiannon was on a complete high and still in a state of shock, she got another call. It was the mother again, explaining that she and her husband had come to a decision. They were going to sue the hospital for making such a huge mistake and for causing them such unnecessary stress. They wanted to know if Rhiannon would advise on this.

The only words that quietly came out of Rhiannon's mouth were "But what about the healing you received?" She hung up and refused to ever speak to the lady again. She was gutted that someone could dismiss the miracle that they had all been honoured to witness. Had the mother forgotten how scared she was when she thought her baby might be seriously ill? So it seemed that when the lady needed to believe, it was ok, but when everything was back to normal, she disregarded that belief.

Rhiannon was deeply affected by this, as was Hannah too. They came to the conclusion that the healing hadn't been for the mother, it had been for the good of the unborn child. They learned a harsh lesson that day about some people's idea of God. To this day that girl is healthy and enjoying life.

Believe my friend. Believe.

Some of You Are Asked to Act as a Channel to Help Heal Spirits

You may know this as rescue work.

Rescue work is commendable stuff. Quietly working without recognition from other humans, there are a lot of people doing this, in your world. I'm not talking about the ghost hunters on your TV shows. I find all that shouting and taunting of lost souls disrespectful actually.

I'm talking about the people who come across a troubled soul that has crossed over, but has not found their way to Heaven's door.

Rescue workers help the soul through the door, so to speak, so they can return home and start again.

First of all let's talk about why this happens to some people when they die.

Well the easiest way I can put it is like this.

Some souls are lost, upset and refusing to leave their life, for whatever reason. Maybe they died suddenly with no warning, or maybe it happened very traumatically and before they were ready and so they refuse to accept it and go to their place of rest. Maybe, they are so worried about the loved ones they have left behind that they try to stay and help as best they can.

Quite often rescue work is simply, passing on an important last message from one of these souls, so they can 'rest in peace'

Ghosts are souls who have stayed living their human life even after death. They don't want to accept, or don't know that they have physically died and just want to live their lives as they have always done, for years. Spirit lives alongside humans everywhere – the worlds are so close. Many, who have not gone over, for whatever reason, are often quite happy staying for a little longer in the life they knew. Remember there is no time in spirit, it is only in your world that you run your life by a 24 hour clock.

The time will eventually come for all of them when, for their own good, they need to be set free and helped to move on. Rescue workers help them to pass over to the right place from the middle ground.

Like I said – this is unrecognised and unpaid, but admirable work.

You can do this from the other side of the world if need be. A soul can travel with thoughts, don't forget, they don't need legs like you guys. They will become attracted to a pure channel – a rescue worker – and beg for help as soon as they realise they can be seen and noticed. This is often quite distressing for the person who is acting as the channel – not knowing why, or who they have suddenly picked up on. However, with a little experience, the entire process can be done in a matter of minutes.

Some Are Here to Help Animals

Animals cannot speak for themselves, yet they are here to learn the same lessons as you humans. They need people to stand up for their rights, speak for them and heal them too.

These people will have been animal mad from a very young age. They are compassionate, gentle and patient beings, who have developed their communication skills with animals over many years.

Thank God for these people I say – not enough of them around.

Some of You Are Here to Simply Experience Earthly Benefits

By this I mean experiencing benefits such as money and human love, for the first time.

These people, quite often, have no interest in the other life, or the true meaning of life, until their later years. Don't judge them – you are not in a position to judge anybody. You all have to start somewhere you know.

Hey, you know that feeling of utter jealousy that you get when you see someone who is successful, rich, or living the good life with every material asset you can possibly wish for? Yeah, well pity them! They are young souls, who are learning the first harsh lesson, that money cannot buy happiness.

You have all been there before, by the way. That's why now; this time around you have a different view on money. Look at the whole planet and see the damage that money has caused on a worldwide scale. Things are changing and changing fast.

"Why do some lucky buggers get to experience the good life then?" I hear you ask. What about the professional footballers, who are driving around in their sports cars and have overflowing bank accounts, or the pop stars who are making a million every second? Don't laugh my advice to you is this – pity them! They have agreed to come round for a hard lesson. Again, it's matters of the heart! Stop looking at the material benefits of their lives and start focusing on the emotional side. They have had to learn that money doesn't buy happiness and trust me that is a painful lesson to learn.

Take a close look at how few friends they have. Bucket loads of money and an entourage of people following them everywhere, but are they real friends, or are they just after the limelight and a piece of the action?

Watch what happens when the money disappears.... and, if the money stays, look at the sadness in their eyes....

Now there are a few well known celebrities who have finally worked out the lesson. Greed has gone and they have realised that life gets better when you give. They have sussed that it's not the money that is making their life happy, but the ability to give to others in need. They have also sussed out, through what are probably very painful experiences that genuine people are brought to them, to support and love them, once they work this lesson out.

There are a few of them that have been used to heal, without even knowing it. What about the musicians with worldwide fame? Their music really does speak volumes to you guys doesn't it? The power of love is portrayed in their words, often helping individuals that the artist will never know about, or get to meet. For that, they are rewarded by having love and comfort in their lives. Don't begrudge them this – be happy for them and watch your life improve too.

So they have been used to channel through music – but let's not forget that the inspiration for their love songs most of the time, is their own pain. So yet another example of having to suffer to be able to heal others....

So, Why Are You Here?

What do your guides want to do with you?
What exactly is YOUR life purpose?

Let's ask them shall we?

Rhiannon bypasses me on this and heads straight to the main man, when she feels like it. She soon comes sliding down the ladder back to me, with her tail between her legs – after having been told the same thing as the last time she asked. She is here to teach. End of!

Meditation

Here is a meditation to get to your highest guide. This top dude won't bother to hold a two-way conversation with you like you're now used to with your everyday guide. Oh no, instead this one answers with one-word answers. Bluntly!

Don't take offence – it is what it is. The energy will feel extremely different. Oh and don't even bother laughing and joking about – you will feel the seriousness when you arrive.

As with any meditation, make sure you are in a safe and comfortable place and you have grounded, protected and opened up your crown chakra.

Get that candle lit.

Spend a few moments focusing on what your question will be, when you get to ask it. I would keep it simple such as "What am I here for?", or "What is my life purpose?"

Sit up in a chair and make sure your legs and arms are uncrossed.

Chant in your head, saying each word with intent – "I wish to connect with my highest guide. I wish to connect with my highest guide. I wish to connect with my highest guide."

Imagine or 'see' a ladder in front of you. Not too tall, instead it's a bit like a step ladder. It is balanced – standing up all by itself without any support, yet it is not wobbling at all. It is sturdy, even though it's in front of you and not leaning against anything.

Study it. Notice what it is made of. Feel it in your mind. Is it smooth cold metal, or is it rough splintered wood? Run your hands down the sides of the ladder and become familiar with it. See how many steps there are up to the top – one, two, three and four.

Now, when you are ready in your mind, see yourself step onto the first rung of the ladder. Put both feet on together. Hold onto the top and see how the ladder hasn't even moved. You are safe.

Look around you. Look left, look right and look behind you in your mind's eye. Remember you are using your third eye here, not your real eyes. You will see souls in spirit, at this level. Take note of who you can see. Do you recognise anyone that has crossed over – your parents, your loved ones, or your friends, maybe? Take as long as you want to say "Hello". Study what they look like, tell them that you love them and accept what they have to say to you in return.

When you are ready, climb up to the next step on the ladder.

On this level you will see your guide to the right hand side of you, smiling at you. Say "Hello" and have a chat, if you wish. Take the time to really study what they look like close up. Now look behind them, you may well catch a glimpse of more guides who work with you. If you do, ask them to introduce themselves. This is your opportunity to see them all.

They will let you know when it is time to go.

Hold firmly onto the side of the ladder and prepare to go up to the next step.

The energy is going to change dramatically now. Become aware of the clouds on the sky line now and, when you are firmly on the third rung; look down first at your guides just below you. They will be looking up and reassuring you, if you feel at all nervous, that it's okay to continue.

Now look around at eye level and you will see you have an angel beside you. This is your very own guardian angel, who has been assigned to you since birth. Don't be alarmed if they are over 8ft tall, this is normal. These are God's messengers and they will help you up to the final level on your ladder. Spend a moment feeling the energy here. It's peaceful, serene, calm and gentle. If your angel speaks to you, you won't just hear the words, but you will feel them in your heart too.

When you are ready – move on to the top of the ladder.

It won't wobble, you are safe. Put both feet on the top rung, steady yourself and then let go and stand tall. Lift your arms above your head and stretch as tall as you can. Look around you – what do you see? You are above the clouds and the feeling of freedom is immense. Your angel is directly below you, keeping you safe. No need to look down; just keep focusing up and around you. Breathe, into your lungs, the fresh clean air.

You will not necessarily see a guide here. You will just hear the answer to your question. Ask firmly "What is my life purpose?", or "What am I here for?"

Accept the first word you hear, or the feeling you get and give thanks.

Stay there for as long as you need and when you feel ready to return, slowly walk down the ladder. As you go down each step, you will see each person you met on the way up.

Bring yourself back to reality and when you are ready, open your eyes.

What word did you hear? Why are you here? Don't try and make sense of it, just accept it.

No, that wasn't the Creator you just heard, that was your highest guide. Think of him as the one who holds the book with your life mapped out in it.

CHAPTER 8
Hearing The Big Man Himself!

If you are considering skipping this chapter, please ask yourself this first. What or who is it that you are channelling that is giving you the ability to help others, with unconditional love?

Woah! Now we have to go back to basics, yet again.

"But I don't believe God is real." you say. Okay!

Are you sure you don't believe in a 'Creator', or are you still battling with the religion and spirituality thing? Are you questioning right and wrong, good and bad, modern or traditional and all that jazz?

Oh no, are you wondering where do you fit in today? What box shall we put you in? Or are you just scared of being judged, by other humans....

He/It, whatever you want to call the Creator, is not angry with you at all. He would love to get a call from you. Why would you think God would not talk to you personally? Oh yes, because you have some things you think he is angry with you for, right?

Religion has instilled this fear into you. Even if you haven't ever believed in Him, you have grown up knowing that the church says – "If you sin, God will not be happy with you and will punish you". Please remember, the religious groups have told you that, not God Himself. He will not punish you. He, more than anyone, is rooting for you to succeed and would love to see you happy. He is the one person who will forgive you for anything – even when you don't forgive yourself....

Maybe you think you are not worthy, or important enough for Him to care about, or to talk to? Mmmmm, we all experience those feelings you know. He is the big Boss that you all worry about, deep down. You wonder about His opinion of you and whether you are in His good books, or not.

You see, He is the Father of all the realms, not just you guys on earth. We all report back to Him and are all His creations. Pretty impressive stuff, eh?

Does that help you to see your guides in a different light? Guides and the souls in the spirit world, as you know it, have a slightly better view of the whole creation thing. They have now experienced life where you are, as well as life where they now are and, quite possibly a lot of other realms too.

This is real progress guys.

I pray with Rhiannon. We both give thanks to the Creator – whatever title, or name you want to give to Him, Her or It. Be it, Divine Love or Energy; just recognise that you should show your gratitude, faith and trust up there to a 'something'. Yet again, a small, but significant way of preventing the old devil called ego coming in.

Every time Rhiannon steps into a church building, a place that she connects with the traditional God that she was brought up to believe in, she breaks down in tears. She is overwhelmed with the feeling of being loved. The one emotion she is dodging desperately, as it brings so much pain for her.

She also still battles with the idea that she will have a lot to answer for when she gets up to Heaven, when she has to explain that she talked to the dead, as a job. See, it takes a lifetime to overcome deep rooted beliefs and fears and ideas that have been put into your mind since childhood.

Oh and she feels small – insignificant, in fact. Touching base with her faith makes her realise how big the picture really is. She is also furious at Him for taking her husband away from her. She can't understand why, after all she does, He would punish her. The truth is He hasn't punished her; He has supported her all the way and sent extra help – in the shape of me.

Sitting quietly and just connecting is a wonderful way of talking to Him. You don't have to speak with words. He can see into your heart. When you are feeling rejection and someone gives you love – it really physically hurts. Let it in, my friend – in your own way.
These days praying is mistaken as 'begging for something', but you don't need to ask for a single thing. You just say "Thank you" for it. It's that simple.

We all know that we should say "Thank you" to Him for what we already have, but how about saying "Thank you" for the things you really want or need, but haven't quite got yet? Why? Because it's another way of having faith and totally trusting and knowing that He will give you what you want, because you simply believe that He will give it to you.

Bingo! Just say "Thank you!"

Some of you feel more comfortable calling it cosmic ordering, or utilising the law of attraction. These are normally the terms used by people who like to think of it as the Universe helping them rather than a Creator. That's cool with me – whatever makes you feel comfortable.

However, don't go asking for stupid things, will ya? Who is the first one to get the blame when it doesn't work out eh?

The funniest one Rhiannon and I have come across is a lady who detailed a long list of her requirements. It went something like this:

A man who is…
Rich
Dark haired
Good looking
Between the age of 45 – 55
Genuine and honest
In love with me

She got it alright. The only problem was that she forgot to mention that she would like him NOT to be married to someone else.

She honestly couldn't understand why the universe had failed her.

We didn't laugh until she had gone – promise.
You don't have to go to the lengths of writing down a list of desires like cosmic ordering books tell you to do, but you do have to realise how powerful you are. You can indeed create everything you want and need in your life. You just have to recognise and appreciate what you have been given. It may not be exactly as you imagined originally.

No, a car isn't going to land on your driveway as a prize, but your job may change or a promotion may be offered, so more money will be in your bank. Then suddenly, you will come across a garage with your dream car on special offer, in the showroom. We will create the impossible for you. Don't you dare sulk at the way it's brought to you, or you will be shown the hard way just how lucky you are. By this I mean that you will suddenly find yourself surrounded by people who are a lot worse off than you.

What do you pray for?

You are able to have everything you want in life – love, money, success, the lot. All you need to do is to believe that you deserve it and trust that it will be given.

Now imagine your guides, who have been told to help you succeed, standing behind you with a clip board, writing down everything you randomly wish for during the day. Because, this is what it's like. Every time you put out intent, or express a need for something, it is noted. All we are trying to do is supply you with all the tools and desires you need to be able to fulfil your life's goal.

So, when you see your neighbour polishing his new wagon or a flash git drives passed in his sports car and you say "Oooh, I wish I had a new car like that!" the thought is written down. When you get invited into a neighbour's house and the feeling of envy runs through you at the sight of their cream carpets and new big screen TV, this has also been noted.

Life does not have to be hard my friend. Think it. See it. Believe it. Achieve it. That's not the same as – think it, believe it and sit back and wait for it. We will meet you half way; remember God helps those who help themselves. The power of the words you use is so strong. If only you knew. Choose your words carefully from now on.

If you were to say "It's not fair, I never have it easy", or "My life is always so hard", guess what we hear? More lessons of hardship are sent your way, my dear. Turn those words around now and say "I love my life", "I am happy", even if it is through gritted teeth – saying those words will bring happy times and good luck.

The damage that negative thoughts and actions have is devastating. Please think before you speak, especially when directing your words at other people. It doesn't matter how bad or nasty someone has been to you – look into their eyes, before you yell back. See the soul inside the human body, for the eyes are the window to it. Think of them as the innocent child they once were and you will see in them what we see.

Send love to everyone you meet, help them along their journey. You can still walk away from the people who don't help you or those who hold you back, but don't wish them negative thoughts. Remember – what goes around comes around. Your life will become harder and more people will be sending you the same negativity right back. Treat others with respect and you will have respect given to you.

Here are the simple rules of what you call karma. I call it common sense. Hurt someone – you will get hurt yourself. Love someone, you will be loved too. Take someone's property, or a girlfriend even and another person will take yours. You may have to wait a pretty long time sometimes for karma to come round, but it always does.

Each time you do something wrong like this, it is almost like you have okayed a particular emotional lesson,. So, to make sure you know how you made the other person feel, we are going to have to make you feel what you have just dished out. Then you can understand it fully.

It works the other way too – do something nice and it comes back tenfold. Try sending positive thoughts out to a bad situation that you know about and the next time you are struggling, things will work out a lot faster for you. Be warned though, it only works like that if you are genuine with your thoughts and intentions of wanting to help someone or something.

So do you attract bad times into your life? No – shit happens, my friend, but you can and will get yourself out of every down turn in life, with a little help from your friends.

CHAPTER 9
Channelling For Other People

Working with your guide to pass on messages for other people is a wonderful thing to do. You will have done this already in life, maybe without knowing you were doing it. Ever had the feeling, when you are giving your opinion or advice to a friend that the words weren't from you? You wonder how the hell you could possibly sound so knowledgeable about a subject you know nothing about – yep you were channelling.

You need to prepare in the same way as you do when channelling for yourself, by grounding, protecting and opening up.

Light your candle, 20 minutes before the client arrives to make it known that any loved ones connected to the person are welcome to come and say "Hello" during your session.

A little tip for you here is to connect to the person you are channelling for. Loop yourself into them when they are sitting down in front of you.

Imagine a thick rope in a figure of eight, connecting the two of you around the waist. This ties you into their energy.

Become aware of how you are feeling physically and emotionally, as you are picking up on your client's feelings now. You almost feel as if you are turning into them. Your usual aches and pains will be gone and instead, you will feel theirs. Sometimes it's not pleasant, I agree, but it is a wonderful way of being able to have compassion and understanding for what they are going through. Another bonus of doing this is to be able to tell the client what you are feeling, which gives them immense trust in you and confidence that you are able to understand them.

Don't look directly at your client. Their facial expressions will put you off – their fear, their worry and that screwed up weird face they make when, at first, they can't take your message. They can all be most off putting. Focus your attention instead on your guide, or their loved ones, who will appear to the side of them.

Say whatever you get. It is not for you to keep, or decide whether to it pass on. If you have been trusted with a message, then pass the damn thing on. Try holding information back, just once and you will regret it. It will bug you for the rest of the day and you will end up having to track down your client and pass it on finally, late at night. If you got the message – you pass on the message, even if it doesn't make sense to you. Your guides are not wrong.

What happens if you see spirit? Say what you see. Describe exactly what they look like or repeat exactly what they say. Again, this is all confirmation, to the client, that they are not alone.

You will all, at least once, have the annoying moment when you can see a loved one in spirit, you describe them in great detail, your client gets excited and then they say nothing. Nothing at all! No message to pass on – you sit there like a lemon willing them to speak. However, sometimes words are not needed. Explain that they are not speaking – never lie or make it up. If you do, your connection will be cut off, out of disgust and you will look pretty stupid.

Now, what if a particular person doesn't come through? The feeling of failure will hit you when the client says "Thank you, but I really wanted my Granny to come today, not my Granddad." Oh charming! I wish the people would understand how much energy it takes the soul of a loved one to come back and make themselves seen and heard. How rude! Would they have said that to their faces, if Granddad turned up at their door when he was alive instead of Granny? No, I don't think so! Don't feel bad and don't apologise – explain that you have no control over who comes to speak – you are just the channel for people to use.

Want to connect with your own loved ones and struggling?

Have a little think about why this could be difficult. So you can channel other people's nearest and dearest by following the normal instructions, but not your own.... Hmmmmm – which emotion is blocking you? Go right back to the beginning few chapters and work out what is preventing you from seeing and hearing your loved one.

If I tell you that Rhiannon saw her husband, as clear as anything, when it was to pass on a message from him to someone else, but it took two years to be able to hear him for herself. Does that give you a clue, as to which emotion is in the way?

It's not their fault for not coming through – it's your fault for trying to channel through an emotion....

Now it's time to correct a myth. It is NOT true that a religious person would not come through a medium, after they have died. Rhiannon has channelled many a priest and vicar in her job. Remember there is no religious divide over here. So, to suggest that a soul who has crossed over, would still disagree with mediums is ludicrous. Telling a client this, is very damaging too. It makes them believe that talking to the dead, through you, is frowned upon.

So why don't some people come through? Well, maybe because they don't want to upset or interfere. It does not mean they are not watching over their loved one and it doesn't mean that you have failed as a channel. Freedom of choice still exists on the other side

84

you know. Maybe, just maybe, your guide has protected you from something that you would not have been able to handle whilst channelling.

Rhiannon has been pushed, just once, to channel a particular person. She managed, through guilt, to push the barriers, wanting to help the lady whom she was reading for. Heavily pregnant at the time, she succeeded and then found herself unable to cope with the energy of the person. Trust that you are not in control of the session with your client, but that your guides know best – every single time!

Now, the message you give to a client, may well be showing what is coming up. Remember we talked about this earlier, in another chapter.

There are two types of readings; one is more of a prediction, which comes about when the client is already on the right path and everything is on track. In this case you will be telling the client what is ahead of them, if they continue and don't go changing their life. They should listen to the reading then sit back, put it to the back of their mind, trust spirit and wait for it to happen. They will be reassured as they are able to tick off each part of the message as it happens.

The second type of reading is a guidance session, almost like a form of counselling. In this case spirit will give direct instructions to change an area or part of life, in order to change things for the better. They are not giving your client a magic solution, there is work to be done and the client has to act on the advice in order to achieve their goals.

The problem with people is that they do not listen to the whole message. They pick out the bits they want to hear and do not follow instruction and then wonder why things don't happen.

So, what about this? In a reading, you have absolutely promised them that success and a better way of life is on its way and you have shown them how to work for it. Then, two months later they call you and say, "But how?" "When?" "It hasn't happened!" Why is this? It is because they have sat on their back sides. They expected it to come to them because a dead person said it was going to happen, but they did nothing to help themselves. They forget the advice you passed on about changing their job, or working hard, or looking for the shop premises. The only bit they latched on to was the money and success at the end of it.

Readings and messages are given to help you better your life. NOT to magically provide you with everything you dream of, without any work.

Advertising your services is totally fine with us. You need to earn your money and pay your bills, just like all the other professions in your world, but be careful of letting the ego sell your trade? No big 'I am's' and claims and, no using your guides to make a quick buck.

We do chuckle at the people who like to list off "I am clairaudient, I am clairsentient and I am clairvoyant." Well done! You forgot to mention you walk with two legs too!

Hopefully, by now, you see that you are no different to the client who has come to you for help. They are just as good as you are at channelling, maybe better. Feel honoured that their guides have trusted you, by allowing you to give them guidance.

Now, there are certain things that you aren't going to get paid paper money for. Being able to work with your guides in a flash, when needed and without any recognition – this should become a way of life for you, especially if you have understood the whole of this book.

Accepting that spirit are around you at all times, should enable you to lead a bit more of a selfless life. You are able to send love, positive thoughts, healing and help from above, to strangers in distress. For example whilst you are driving, but can't stop, you can send your powerful thoughts of love and assistance to the victims of a car crash that you have witnessed.

In fact, you can send love to anyone and any situation that catches your attention – without recognition. We will know and we will help you to be compensated. If the money has dried up, the customers aren't coming to you, but you have spent time and energy selflessly and anonymously helping others, you will soon see trade pick up.

So, the next time a homeless man asks you to spare some change, give him everything you have. Remember, this is a whole new way of life – trusting that you are being provided for, by your guides.

Always close down and cut the ropes after each client. Cut ties and keep yourself safe.

Oh and don't be afraid to tell us to bugger off every now and then. If you stay open, we will assume you are fit for work. We understand you need time in your earthly role to have fun and focus on relationships with other humans. You are allowed to be silly and childlike – you don't have to be perfect all the time. Only when channelling!

Now I know that at least one of you, reading this, is wondering if we are around during private moments in your life.... Okay, time for ME to confess. I have walked in ONCE when Rhiannon and her husband were in bed, but in my defence I had an urgent message to pass onto her about her shop. She was grateful, Dave however wasn't ☺.

CHAPTER 10

Rhiannon's Bit!

I hope Brian's book has helped you. We would both love for you to experience working together with your guide, as we do.

I have a lot of different guides, who I have the honour of working with, but none quite like Brian. They don't speak to me really, unless it is to give an instruction.

I have spent a lot of time getting to know Brian. I can see his face, his skin, and his coarse grey whiskers, so clearly. Seeing the squint in his eyes, when he talks to me seriously, lets me know he loves me.

The clothes he wears are well…. unique. He is like a leprechaun in a suit and he has a range of clothes that are just as funny as his walk. When we do clairvoyant nights together he likes to wear a velvet jacket with a multi coloured bow tie and he cartwheels down the aisle to get to the person I need to give the next message to.

I love his facial expressions. He makes me laugh out loud. I recognise what mood he is in by his walk or the way he struts towards me. He is a joker too and watching him skidding into the room at times makes me spin round and roar with laughter.

When my husband was alive, he struggled to come to terms with Brian being in our lives. He couldn't see him, but had so much proof that he was real. In a strange way he was, at times, jealous of another man being able to have a private conversation with his wife – until he came to see that Brian was there to help, not hinder. It helped when Brian's advice saved us money, time and effort and Dave realised that he was on our side.

A powerful moment that I remember was the first time I touched Brian's hand. We actually both got an electric shock from it. The skin on his knuckles looked so sore and red and cracked and I couldn't believe it was so clear to me. I ran my fingers over his knuckles to see if I could physically feel what I could see. After the shock of the electric shock, we both screamed with laughter and then he squeezed my hand. It was then I knew he was real.

I knew he cared deeply for me from early on. He seemed so sad when he was singing to me 'No More I love You's' from the Annie Lennox song. I didn't understand what he was trying to say to me, but it felt like he was trying to tell me in code. He would look away with such sad eyes and I was left wondering who was going to be leaving me.

A few months later my husband was diagnosed with pancreas cancer, when my son was about 6 months old. I understood then that Brian wasn't allowed to tell me straight out, but when we were alone, he was letting me know and trying to prepare me, in the only way he could. I couldn't have gotten through the death of my husband without Brian.

I simply adore him. I have come to trust him with my life. That doesn't mean to say I like everything he says. Actually, if truth be known, he annoys me so much at times, but I know he has my best interests at heart. I trust him implicitly now.

We argue like a married couple. He gets so cross with me when I don't listen or act upon his words. He leaves me alone when I am having a meltdown and want to be miserable, or if I ask, he will just simply sit with me and hold my hand.

We have cried together, he feels my pain and I feel his. I have had long conversations about his life's experiences and he has carried me through mine. I understand why he is wary of men, because in each of his human lives, he has been treated very badly by a lot of them.

We have giggled about finding out we used to be married to each other once, and yes, we were both dwarves. That stopped me laughing at his size instantly. Apparently our married life was as funny as our relationship is now. Him being right and me thinking I am right....

He warns me about other people and tells me what is about to happen. He can't make me listen though. He gets angry with me and frustrated and starts shouting obscenities, which makes me shout back at him. I always end up having to be the one to apologise when he is proved right.

He has introduced me to his family. His quiet, gentle, long suffering wife Rosie is lovely. She has had to put up with him being with me, day in and day out, for years now. He has shown me his children. They had 6 little ones when he first came into my life.

My children have been woken up in the night, on many occasions, by Brian's children playing with their toys and the guitar in their bedroom. One of my daughters has even seen Rosie at her bedroom door, beckoning to her children to get them out of the room.

One day I was lying in bed in the daytime feeling very sorry for myself, refusing to get up and live my life. Brian appeared and signalled for me to stay quiet. He then waved his arm to Rosie to come over to me. Imagine my shock as the two of them carefully clambered up onto my bed holding a bundle wrapped up in traditional swaddling. They had come to show me their new addition to the family.

That was not only magical, but also a huge lesson for me. It taught me that Brian really is in a different realm to us, not in spirit world as we know it – where we go after we die. He is in another world and is living right here and now, just like us. We are communicating and working together from different realms – for the same purpose.

I have seen Brian meet up with my husband Dave, after he died in 2009. I saw the two of them sitting down and talking about me. I knew Brian was telling Dave what was coming up for me and his children, now we were on our own. I am so pleased that Dave could finally get to see and talk to Brian himself. To this day, the two of them work together to help me and they're actually good friends now!

CHAPTER 11
And Finally....

Below is a copy of some of Brian's views and some question and answer sessions that we have had together. Some serious and some funny – we got bored, sorry!

Brian's Views on Soup

Why do you mush up your food like that? Not good.

Brian's Views on Love

Powerful drug, isn't it? One that can make you do really stupid things, yet one that that makes you see the whole world differently. It's a beautiful place, when you have someone to share it with and a sad old hole when you are alone.

There's nothing better than the love of a good woman, like a mother.

Brian's Views on Work

It's pointless unless, you love it. Work should not be a chore, it should be a pleasure. How many times have we had to tell people, in their readings, to change their job to do something they dreamt of when they were young? Follow your dreams and all will be fine. Too many people go into jobs because of other people's opinions, some because of money and yet others because of lack of self confidence. I say that anything is possible when you are determined. Just look at how ill people become when they are stuck in a job they

hate. Like me by the way – it's such a chore working with you
Rhiannon…. I jest – a little!

Brian's Views on Smart Arses

Feel sorry for them that's what I say. They are only like that because
they are falling short in other areas of their lives. Like personality.

Brian's Views on Fairies

Beautiful things, but I couldn't eat a whole one. Never trap one
though – they turn nasty. I should know – I have the scars to prove
it.

Brian's Views on Religion

Woah! Do not get me started. Too late – I am gonna love this one.

There is a God. He made us, but not in seven days. The bible was
written by people not God. Yes, Jesus was God's son and he came
down to earth – just like the rest of you. You are all God's sons and
daughters. Jesus was sent down to try and sort out the bloody mess
this world was in, back then, with all the arguing, war, rules and
destruction that mankind had made. It didn't work. Well it did for a
bit, but it soon went back to the way it was.

However, by sending Jesus, God showed that He was real and He
showed what every one of his children was capable of, by sending
his son into the firing line.

You all use about one sixth of your brain – what do you think the rest
is for? Filling a gap? Padding? No, you are all capable of doing

what Jesus did – healing, hearing God and living by his example. He tried desperately to show us the right way to live, be kind to thy neighbour and all that. Did we listen? Nope. By the way, he is still trying, but in different ways and through different people. Take a look around you and note the people that shine. They are not all Mother Teresa's (though she was an amazing woman, wasn't she?), they are normal people, living around your area. They go that extra mile for others without expecting something back.

You don't have to go to church to be religious. Church has been ruined by mankind. People seem to take the bits they like out of each religion and that's fine, absolutely fine. Believe what you want to believe and stick to it. As long as you don't hurt other people, judge them, or inflict your beliefs onto them, in a nasty controlling way, then it's all good. Lead a good, simple life and do what you hear in your heart – for that is where God is – smack in the middle of you.

Get stuck at anytime, just call out to Him and ask for His help. He always answers, maybe not in the way you want at first, but He always answers. For those of you who are reading this and shaking their head, saying "Well He doesn't bloody answer me" – you are not listening. Don't use the lugs stuck on the side of your head, your heart and your gut whilst you are waiting for His answer.

So, the problem with religion in this day and age is whichever one you choose to follow and believe in, they always seem to want to control you. So I say, don't pick a flipping religion, create your own rules of living, your own code and your own standards and, stick to them. By the way, the Ten Commandments *were* taught by Jesus and make a good basis from which to build your own standards. Just saying….

Brian's Views on Early Mornings

Not impressed.

Brian's Views on Old People

Bloody love them. Start having respect for them will you please?
They should be looked up to. They know a damn sight more than
you guys, as they have lived a lifetime before you. Everything you
have done, they have done first. Make sure you teach your kids
about history. Those plonkers who say that history is not necessary
because it is in the past and the future is what matters, need a brain
transplant. History is the whole reason your future is the way it is.

'Old people's homes' are a bloody disgrace. Here, in my world, old
people are treated like wise ones and you on earth should be doing
the same thing.

Brian's Views on Dieting

Waste of bloody time if you ask me. It wouldn't be necessary if you
all ate a healthy diet in the first place. Why are you women so
interested in looking like a bloody twig in any case? A bit of what
you fancy doesn't do you any harm, but in moderation, of course. If
you listen to your body's needs, you will find that it tells you what it
wants – cravings I think you call them.

Ever get the urge to down a whole pint of pure orange juice? That
would be your liver calling and what about the need for some fresh
veg, after a few weeks of eating carbs? You know what I am talking
about, especially you ladies, who are more in tune with their bodies
than any man I have seen in a long time. The golden rule to follow,
if you are clever is – if God made it, it's good for you. If it's been

tampered with by mankind, it's full of shit that you don't want in your body. Well you did ask....

The bottom line is, if it grew in the ground or on a tree and it hasn't been sprayed with human made concoctions, then it's good for you.

Brian's Views on Adoption

Thank God for the kind hearted people who adopt. Society should drop all the silly rules about who can and can't change a child's life. All a child needs is love, food and shelter and there are so many people who would willingly give that, if there wasn't such a rigmarole to get through.

Brian's Views on the Prison System

Yep, your system is really working isn't it? Of course, locking people up and letting them mix with hardened criminals and the insane, is the answer. Well done guys. Whoever thought of that one must be really proud of themselves. For God's sake – obviously the totally dark characters, need to be away from society, but honestly? What about the pick pockets and petty thieves?

You won't like my suggestion, but I don't care. Take time out to look into the childhood of each prisoner and try and work out why they ended up like they did. Then, put them in a holiday camp and get them some therapy, just as you would a child or a bereaved friend.

Brian's Views on War

Well, it's all about ownership, isn't it? My land, my people, my oil! If you all learned to share the bread and fish, it wouldn't happen would it? Now, when countries pull together and PROTECT themselves from one bad egg, that's impressive. Fighting for peace, sounds wrong, but it makes sense, as a last resort.

Brian's Views on Farts

They still make me laugh at my age. They show God has a sense of humour, if you ask me. There is nothing you can do to stop them from coming and, the people that say they never fart, are downright liars. It is one thing that the body does all by itself that causes great entertainment for everybody in earshot. They definitely get my vote!

Now, burping is nearly as funny, yet another bodily function that is free entertainment for kids. You guys reading this and frowning – lighten up a bit and, as I have been quoted as saying, on many an occasion, "Act your shoe size, not your age!"

Brian's Views on Football

Ha ha ha ha ha ha ha ha ha ha ha ha. Prefer a good game of fairy kicking, personally.

Brian's Views on Western Medicine and Hospitals

There are wonderful souls who have come down to train in medicine and to heal the sick. They are undiscovered angels. They really are. They are, if you like, the chosen ones. They came to give healing

97

when a human body fails itself, or suffers in an accident. We, up here, commend the work of such souls.

However, my beef is with the drug companies. It seems to be one huge, money making scam, rather than an aid to heal the sick. We approve of the medication invented and used to heal the sick in genuine cases, but there is a lot wrong with the way tablets and drugs are being dished out to all and sundry. Tablets actually cause other problems and dependencies that then need further drugs to combat the new problems.

The body is an amazing thing and it is equipped with tools to heal itself, if allowed. Operations and drugs, when necessary, get my complete approval, but the drug companies inventing new ones every day, to get people hooked, is another story altogether. I am sorry to say, it's money, money, money, with too many people. There are not many guys, who invent something and share it with the world, because they want to help with the problems, they just smell money.

I wish pharmaceutical companies would first weigh up the side effects of the drugs they produce and I wish they would be honest about the impacts that could be caused by their products. In fact, they do know, but they just choose not to share those facts with you. So, I wish that people would look more closely, before they take the drugs, to see what the true effect of the tablets will be on other parts of the human body.

Brian's Views on Heaven

Beautiful place – can't wait until you're here with us. We have a party planned.

Does everyone go there Brian?

Yes, eventually.

There is a place that you go to after passing from your world. It is for the 'in-betweenies' shall we say, the ones who are still learning their lessons and want to go back down to learn all over again. Heaven is the final resting place for the complete soul who has finished all their journeys. It's fab, trust me and nothing to worry about – no niggling problems like money to argue over.

Brian is it wrong to talk to people who have passed over? The church says it is a sin, but you talk to me? Am I, or are we, sinners then?

So, do you really think I would be doing it so publicly with you if it were wrong? Stupid question girl, but I see why you are asking it here. No it is not a sin. Spirit and humans need to work together from our two worlds to try and help one another, as we have done for many centuries.

Guides have been assigned to work alongside you on earth – it's our job to help you make the right choices. So, each and every one of you has a guide over here, though not everyone can hear them, or see them. Maybe you don't need to because it would be a hindrance, or even scare you. Others however, like you Rhiannon, need to show the world that there is a bigger picture than maybe people first thought.

By the way, this is nothing new – guides have been working with you on earth since day one. Thank God they have stopped burning at the stake, eh?

Brian, what would your advice be to us parents?

As tempting as it is to tell these kids what to do and when to do it, that's not exactly our role in their lives, is it?

Oh, come on, admit it! It is a damn sight quicker to tell 'em what needs to be done, rather than the other option, of letting them find out for themselves. However, the truth is, they need to learn from mistakes – their mistakes, just like we did. Yes, yes, I know, we do it because we love them and don't want to see them making the same mistakes that we did.

Control freaks – that's what parents on earth should be called. The lot of them! Even the hippy chick ones, who like to think that they are giving their child freedom of choice, though they are, in fact, still inflicting their choices and preferences on their little offspring.

The hardest thing to do is to let your child go and watch them fall. Remember when they first started to walk? They let go of the yoghurt covered sofa and promptly fell flat on their arses, but they bounced back, got up and tried all over again. So why isn't it easy to let them fall flat on their arses later on in life - in the bigger lessons?

Because....................... it's all about control! Sorry to be blunt, but by writing this book, you just kinda knew, I wouldn't be holding back didn't you? When everything else has gone tits up in your life, such as your dreams, your career and your relationships, at least you have your kids to try and live your ideas through eh?

Of course, children are also seen as something that you own, something to be proud of. We see them as our very own creation that others haven't got. You just need to visit a playgroup or coffee morning, to see the mothers competing over who's child looks better,

100

walks first, wears the designer baby grow, talks first – the list is endless.

So let's just smash out another myth right now. Children aren't your property. You do not own them. You have been trusted to raise them for someone else – our Creator. They are adult souls just like you, but they are starting their journey from scratch again, as you did many moons ago. If you keep this in mind, parenting will be a lot easier for you.

You have been chosen by your children to raise them. We all choose our life path. We cannot guarantee other people's reactions, or actions, along the way, but we choose the lessons we want to learn and perfect, each time round. You also choose who to learn the lesson with i.e. your parents, your brothers, your sisters and your friends.

Mmmmm, so I can hear you asking "Why the hell would a child choose a bad parent, one who batters them or neglects them?" Well, let me get one thing straight – they didn't ask for their parents to behave this way towards them. However, they may well have asked to learn a lesson about certain emotions such as hate, fear and betrayal and so on.

Because you see, my friend, that is all you are here to learn and experience – all the different emotions. The good ones and the bad ones!

Here is one for you to enjoy Mum's and Dad's. This is a frequently used kid comment, which is made when their backs are up against the wall and they feel trapped and have no lippy answer left – then they hit you with "I didn't ask to be born!!!" My advice, to respond to all the star signs, is – "Oh yes you bloody did!!!" Enjoy your moment and think of me :) – you deserve it!

101

That brings me onto another thing for you parents who beat yourself up with guilt at not being able to provide the best for your children. Maybe there's not enough damn paper money, maybe you worry about the effects of a divorce, or your choices in life and how that has affected the child's choices. Stop and think about how your child has progressed as a soul, instead of how they have suffered, in your eyes.

A couple splitting up could mean a change of home or kids witnessing arguments and so on. Maybe this all helps to strengthen the child and prepare them for adult life. Maybe, just maybe, it has shown them a glimpse of the real world, instead of the rose tinted world you had dreamt of, for your child.

If the child has suffered greatly and you really cannot see any positive outcome from this, then please take comfort in knowing that the lesson was a necessary one, preparing them for their emotional journey ahead. You never know, maybe they needed to see love from both angles, to help them in their own relationships, during adulthood. We all need to see and feel rejection and neglect in one way or another, before we can really appreciate what love is.

Want to be a good parent? Then do your research. Would you buy a car without checking out a few facts first? No, of course not! Then why do we go into parenting without checking out a few essentials first?

My first bit of advice to all new parents is; check the bloody star sign of the baby you have just signed up for. A star sign gives you a little insight into what you have let yourself in for. It gives you a few little hints as to how the wee child will see life and also, what lesson they have come to learn.

Water Signs

Pisces, Scorpio and Cancer

They are cute, sweet, cuddly and all about love, love, love. Water signs are an adorable species when they are little, but a bloody nightmare, when they grow up and find love with someone else. You will be constantly telling them to toughen up and stop wearing their heart on their sleeve.

However, don't forget, they are here, this time round, to learn about emotional issues that affect the old ticker. So, their soft loving and forgiving nature is a blessing and it is your job to help them use these qualities. Though it's easier said than done, my friend! It is very tempting to shout at them to stop being too emotional and crying over breaking up with friends at primary school, but really, what you need to do is help them work through their feelings and especially, to be able to put into words the emotions that they are experiencing.

Fire Signs

Aries, Sagittarius and Leo

These sprogglings are feisty little buggers. They know exactly what their internal fire is telling them to do and they are born with passion and determination for life. You also need to know that these kids have been round a few times before and have, let's say, unfinished business with the world. They ain't gonna fail a second time round!!!

It is tempting indeed to shout louder than them in an argument and just give orders with punishments, if rules are broken – anything for an easy life. However, that isn't helping them grow is it? No. It just makes them even feistier and even more determined. Hee hee hee, this category brings a smile to my face.

Old souls the lot of them – just remember that.

Air Signs

Gemini, Libra and Aquarius

They are serious and intelligent brain boxes. Yes, they really do know more than you and their brain is highly acute even at the age of two. Oh, how it makes me laugh at the thought of a balding, aging parent trying to control one of these. Now give me a fire sign kid any day...........!!!

Helping with the homework (though you don't have to do it for them) and giving them attention and answers to their many questions may be exhausting, but it is necessary for these little nippers to develop very quickly.

Your job as a parent to one of these souls is to help them advance to their chosen career. It's all about the brain. They are here to bring something to the material world and succeed in business and expansion for their world. Oh how proud you will be when they turn out to be a credit to society. Just think of it that way, when you are pulling your hair out in the early days. Do not be afraid to admit that you do not have a clue what the answer is, to their question. Just find a way for them to find it out themselves, with one of the many resources that the world has available these days.

Earth Signs

Taurus, Capricorn and Virgo

Aaaawwwww, they are so sweet. Do not rush these kids. They will infuriate you with their rituals and ways, but for God's sake do not rush them. They are here to be able to fully appreciate what the material world has to offer. Let them enjoy the pleasures in life, which maybe you know aren't all that important – what with the poverty figures around the world. Nevertheless, they are part of the earth sign experience. These kids need to fully take in everything they see and learn at their own pace. They are very clever too, but they like to make sure they have it absolutely 100% correct before they commit, or move on to the next lesson.

Patience is a virtue with these kids, especially if you are a busy multi-tasking parent.

If you could see kids like I do from this angle, it's hilarious. From the moment they are born there is a huge adult size soul trying to fit into its new shell, which is approximately 54cms tall. They are trying to get used to making the human shell work for them. Highly amusing, I tell you.

What makes me laugh so bloody hard is watching you planning your child's life in advance. Not a good idea, no matter what star sign. Period!

"My son is going to be a doctor, you know. As I am, my father was and his father before him" and so on.... Get yourself ready to be disappointed. Maybe your son doesn't WANT to be a doctor? Yes, you may have convinced him, with guilt that he would be letting the family tradition down, if he doesn't follow this path. You have saved and gone without yourself for years, on the basis that the money would be needed for medical college fees. You may well have won the argument, but, don't be surprised, a few years down the line, when he is miserable and blames you for it, because he didn't fulfil his dream of becoming an entertainer.

Support, that's a good thing to give. Be honest and admit that you don't understand why the hell he or she would want to become a dairy farmer, but investigate the idea with them. Don't ever be embarrassed of your child's choices, if they can't rely on you for support, they really haven't got much going for them have they?

Rules, that's what helps in this parenting lark. Kids actually need to know their boundaries. No means no and, yes means yes and, maybe means, if you are lucky there is a slim chance you may be happy with my answer kid! If a child reads mixed messages from you, then you can't blame them for pushing their luck or not listening to you. You only have yourself to blame, I am afraid.

From a young age, they need to learn that when Mum shouts "Stop", as they are about to run into the middle of a busy road, she should be listened to. So, when a child asks for something and the answer is no, don't bloody let them run to Dad, or another adult, to try for a different answer.

Do not let them find a wedge or crack between the two of you – stick tight together and join forces. Work as a team. Back each other up and that also means, do not argue with your partner, about their parenting skills, in front of the kid. That is showing the kid a way in between the two of you. Wait until the kid is out of ear shot, for goodness sake and then air your grievances. Just don't do it in front of the kid, because that is knocking the family sync out of place, by making the child more important that the adult.

Remember that kids are born like a blank book. The parents write the pages.

I love to hear laughter in your homes. Laughing is so good for the soul you know. It's healing, healthy and gives you a sense of freedom. Sometimes, when there is nothing left to do, after you have reached the point of despair, because your plans have gone right out of the window, try laughing instead of shouting or getting frustrated and angry. Just step back and look at the situation from the outside and laugh. Try it – trust me, it works.

Security for a child is vital. No, I am not talking about padlocks, chains and burglar alarms. I am talking about trust, touching and cuddles. Holding a child's hand gives them the sense of safety and security, even when words don't come easily to you. These little nippers look to you for all the answers in the world. In a situation when you feel nervous and scared, when you don't know what's going to happen or what the answer will be, just holding their hand is enough to let them feel that they can trust you.

There is nothing worse than being a kid with parents who bloody know it all. The truth is though, that every single parent has been where the kid is about to tread – way, way before. Sharing this fact with your children is good. It shows them that you are human too, that you have lived and walked a similar path and have made choices and mistakes too. It is so important to admit your mistakes and to be able to laugh about them with your child. Lie to the rest of the world, if you have to, but not to your children, not if you expect them to respect you and listen to you.

Do you remember being small yourself and highly agitated when your parents seemed to think they know best? They were giving advice on your boyfriend or girlfriend choices. Do you remember thinking "You have never been in this boat before, just shut up"? It's hard to picture your parents as kids; in fact you honestly believe they were just born as parents, not as kids. Remember that when giving advice to a child. Always chip in with a few stories of how it happened to you, making them realise you are human too.

To round off my lecture I want to say that the best thing to come out of your journey together with these kids is friendship. That should be your aim at the end of it all, when they leave your nest, fly off and build their own one. You will have equipped them well enough to start their own adult life and in turn become a parent themselves.... and, your reward? It is a true friend with whom you have travelled a long journey. You have experienced the rough and the smooth paths together and you have both felt the turns, the bumps and the road covered in thin ice. If you are lucky enough to have survived this journey together, you will have made a great friend, who knows you better than any other friend you will ever have the pleasure to meet.

Oh and get out quick before the grandchildren appear. You don't have to do it all over again, unless of course, you are a glutton for punishment and fancy doing it one more time.

Brian – are angels real?

Of course they are. They are a totally different being though, a different species altogether. They work as God's messengers. He is a busy bloke and they are like his helpers. They 'fly' and I use that word loosely, between the two worlds, making sure all is okay. When miracles happen in your world, it is often thanks to an angel stepping in, especially in the case of near misses etc. They keep you safe.

Okay, do we get reincarnated?

Well seeing as you know damn well that we used to be married to each other, you know that the answer is yes. However, for the benefit of the readers – yes, you do get to come round to experience life on earth more than once. How many times in total is different for each one of your souls – you choose that. Each trip is for you to learn an emotion, that's all. If you don't succeed, then you can come down again and learn it in a different scenario.

Now let me guess, the next thing you are going to want to know about is soulmates right?

Well, in a way, I was going to ask you if we choose the people we learn the lesson with?

Soulmates are just that – your mates, your friends. You have met them before and yes you have chosen to have them with you again. Ever had that feeling, when you meet someone for the first time that you have known them for years? Of course you have, well, that's a soulmate. They're not always a lover mind you, before you get confused. Soulmates are your best friends, your siblings, your parents – anyone who is there to support you on your journey this time round.

Many times you swap roles too. So, where the first time round, you had a mother/daughter relationship, maybe this time round it's a daughter/mother relationship, or even a husband and wife one. Yes, before you ask, you can change genders! You are a gender free soul that can choose to be a man or a woman, depending on the lesson you are here to learn.

So you can easily see why sometimes you fight with your nearest and dearest eh? Supposing your daughter used to be your mother, in your past life and she doesn't agree with the way you are taking the lead? You fight like cat and dog because subconsciously she remembers that she used to take the lead.

Power fighting couples who the rest of the world can see shouldn't be together, could possibly have chosen to fall in love with each other in this lifetime, to sort out a long standing dispute. You have all lead a tangled and interesting past together you know, but that is impossible for you guys to appreciate until you get up here. I must say, it is sometimes funny to watch.

What about the scenario where the wife used to be the husband's mother? In this lifetime she has carried on the unconditional love that she had for her little boy, as his mother. Now as the wife, she dotes on her advantage-taking husband and just seems to put up with the fact that he expects her to do everything for him.

Okay here's a killer question for you – do aliens exist?

Well, what do you mean by aliens? If what you are in fact asking is are there other races out there, species other than you humans on earth? The answer is yes. You are talking to me for starters. There are lots of different 'beings' and most can not been seen by the human eye. I hope that tells you that you lot aren't the most superior out of the bunch....

Will they hurt us?

I repeat, you lot aren't more superior. Why the hell would they want to hurt you? They aren't into owning, destruction or throwing their weight around like humans.

What about gay marriages and relationships?

You, as a soul, are not male or female. A soul has no gender. You then choose a male or female body to equip you for the lesson you are here to learn. So what happens if your soulmate this time round has chosen the same sex as you? You cannot switch off the connection you have had together, which has carried you through various lifetimes. Therefore it is not shocking news that two men or two women can fall in love with each other. The only problem is that it causes a huge stir with the rest of society – you know the ones who are so damn perfect that they are in a position to be able to judge others? Hmmpphhh.... Cast the first stone and all that.

So is being bi-sexual normal then, you wonder? Well of course it is. Think back to where I explained about how you know your soulmates from past lives. You can connect with other souls easily, regardless of whether they are male or female this time round. It's not a case of something gone wrong with the making of the body, it is not a hereditary 'problem', nor is it wrong. It is two souls learning to love each other and needing to be together, in that chapter of their life.

Society has got a lot to answer for – it makes me so mad. People who believe that it is okay for them to judge other people's lives, should take a long hard look at themselves first, if you ask me.

What's your advice on marriage these days then?

Sacred, that's what it should be, but, you guys have such a throw away system these days – nothing lasts five minutes with you, you don't savour anything. Your whole life is based on chuck it away and buy new. If you are not happy with something, you change it, but you guys don't seem to give anything five minutes. If you have a piece of technology that works fine and a newer model is brought out, you seem to absolutely need to throw away the old one and get the new model. If you don't like your dinner, you chuck it when you have had enough instead of keeping it for the next day. It's a tragic life style and you seem to have taken on the same attitude towards a marriage.

Rough patches should be worked through, not used as an opportunity and excuse to be able to give up and throw the marriage away. Talking is the answer to everything, oh and listening. Too many people don't even attempt to do this with their partner. They assume they know what the answer or solution is going to be, so they don't even ask the bloody question. This leads to secrets, confusion, anger, fear and a whole lot more negative emotions and this causes wedges between the two people.

Marriage is designed to create families and units. All families have problems, as we all know only too well, but you can't just give up and walk away.

Now, I am not saying that you have to stay in an unhappy marriage – no way would I say that. You have been equipped with an amazing tool – freedom of choice. No one, absolutely no one, can tell you what to do; you have to make your own choices in life. So, if you are unhappy and do not love another person, then you should not be with them. If you struggle with walking away because you will hurt someone, then think on this – is it okay to hurt you? You are clearly here to learn guilt this time round.

Before you ask, no I do not have a problem with divorce – it is perfectly acceptable and should be freely available for when it is necessary. Let's face it, you guys are living a hell of a lot longer than people did when marriage was invented. Back then people died at the age of 30 roughly, but life expectancy has more than doubled now!!!! However, having said that – divorce is being used by too many of you as an easy way to opt out and this is sad to watch from afar. Divorce should be a final option, not a decision made due to anger, or boredom.

Work your bloody problems out, like the grown-ups you are.

Brian, thank you for letting me share your words publicly.

No, thank you, Rhiannon for writing it down for all to see.

My pleasure, darling. Do you think we are going to get into trouble for writing some of these things? What if people don't agree?

Now when have I ever cared what anyone thinks apart from you? You and me are here to do a job for Him up there and that's what we're doing chick. He never said it was going to be easy.

Very true Brian, very true. Love you buddy xx

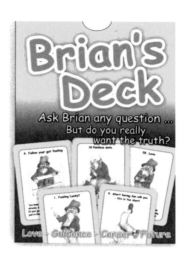

Brian's Deck
Can You Handle the Truth?

Brian Copthorne the little man known for being Rhiannon Faulkner's spirit guide who gives amazingly accurate predictions, is now able to be at your beck and call with this wonderful inspiration deck.

He tells people like it is and doesn't waste time messing around with airy fairy answers.

Rhiannon, best known for creating The Faulkner Tarot Deck has now devised this beautiful set of cards, allowing us all to channel Brian for expert advice.

Brian's Deck by Rhiannon Faulkner
ISBN 978-0-9565388-0-2

WAGONS AND CARTS

David Viner

SHIRE 🍂 LIBRARY